MY
PASSION
FOR CARP

ANDY LITTLE

BEEKAY PUBLISHERS

Other carp fishing titles by Beekay Publishers

First published in 1992
© BEEKAY PUBLISHERS
WITHY POOL
BEDFORD ROAD
HENLOW CAMP
BEDS SG16 6EA
ENGLAND

ISBN 0 947674 41 1

Printed in the UK

CONTENTS

Front cover: Andy at Salagou, France.
Back cover: Andy with his 41.9

Drawings by Brian Atkins. Photographs by the author and friends.

Foreword

There will be few carp anglers who read this book who haven't heard of the author, Andy Little, for Andy holds a place at the very top of the sport and has done so for some years. His catches alone make most people froth at the mouth, and his regular writings, be it the weekly 'Anglers' Mail' column, or articles published in the U.K. angling magazines, not to mention numerous works in the European press, have made him a household name.

But what makes him so special? How does he catch so many carp, including some absolute whoppers, almost at the drop of a hat? I suppose I should know, for during these last ten years I've been close to Andy and fished – on and off – with him during this time. The uncanny high ratio of bites to the amount of time he's actually fishing, is something I can't explain away, but it happens – often.

Once we fished a water together, although the 'going' swim was too small to let two people fish side by side. During the summer we caught many carp from this spot. I myself fished well during this time, hardly losing any fish through breakage or failed hook-hold. Fishing for more or less the same amount of time as Andy, he still managed to bank ten more good carp than I did – that's the only time I've come close to his amazing carp catching skills – before or since.

His list of big carp captures is impressive enough, the total of all carp caught is vast, but in the midst of all this, his enthusiasm, love of carp, his fishing and the sport in general is so strong that sometimes he leaves me gasping for breath. You see he's never lost sight of, or the thrill of catching carp. I remember him one day landing a 13lb mirror carp that had pretty scaling; however, he was in total awe of this ordinary sized but beautifully scaled fish and waxed lyrical for several minutes. That's one example of why he's still 'carp crazy'.

Within the pages of this volume you'll find chronicled Andy Little's carp fishing exploits from its beginnings – by the end you'll realise why, when asked about his remarkable ability, I refer to Andy as: 'A Matchman who goes carp fishing!'

Chris Ball

Introduction

I suppose looking back at how long this book has taken to put together, and just how many carp Andy's had, it's amazing we managed to condense it to a publishable length.

Without wishing to reveal Andy's age, I think it's fair to say that he's been carp fishing for a long, long time. Anglers have come and gone: in fact, organisations have come and gone, in that time, but Andy still continues to put carp on the bank week in, week out. From his early days on his local stillwaters and rivers to his Cassien exploits, Andy's infectious enthusiasm for catching carp has inspired and excited us all, young and old. I would guess that at least 90% of people who carp fish today have read about him or watched his famous slide shows.

When you come to the end of the last chapter, sit back – or, even better, flick through the book again – and see just how many carp waters Andy has fished and come to terms with. Johnsons, Savay, Cut Mill, Burton, Frensham Minor, Longfield, Yateley, Kingfisher, Willow Park, Burghfield, Redmire, Darenth, Brooklands and so on – the list seems endless. Small or large, hard or impossible, his persistence, original thinking and common sense approach has enabled him to break down barriers and shatter records. Whilst many other name anglers of today have had success on a restricted number of waters, Andy's overall record stands favourable comparison with anyone else's.

My involvement with Andy goes back to the mid 80's when, as a struggling youngster, I made my way down from Yorkshire to Andy's Surrey home via our old friend British Rail. Laden to the gunnels with tackle for a couple of days on the bank, I raised more than a cursory look, especially on my return journey coated to the eyelids in carp slime. Despite not knowing me from Adam (whoever he is), Andy was good enough to take me into his home, treat me as a friend, and put me onto some good winter carp waters. As a starstruck youngster I fished that first winter with Andy and we had considerable success no matter where we fished.

Whilst Andy is indeed a carper of extreme keenness he is, first and foremost, a family man. Each time we fish together I always take time out to see Jeanie and their children Mark and David. From young children to little boys I've seen the lads grow and I now have a knowledge of everything from Thomas the Tank Engine to Mutant Ninja Turtles! On those cold winter nights when it can be a pain to be out there doing it, it's nice to see another aspect of life, an aspect far more important than any part of carp fishing.

As we go through the 1990's, I'm sure Andy's name will continue to dominate carp fishing. I'm only too glad that he has allowed me to share his knowledge and help. Our sessions together are always a pleasure, and from feeding a swim correctly, to pacing yourself in a session, to appreciating carp of all sizes, Andy has helped me in many ways. Hopefully, the book you have before you will help you in your fishing today – I am sure it will.

To end, my friends are always asking me just how good Andy is as an angler. Well, that's a hard question; surely his record speaks for itself. If not, I'll leave you with this thought; if I was asked to catch a carp to save my life, I know who I'd hand the rod over to – Andy Little.

Read on ...

Julian Cundiff

1 — The Early Years

It's difficult to say where it all started. I certainly started fishing at a very young age, but not specifically for carp; that was more of a progression than a defined step. My father was a very keen all round specimen hunter who fished virtually every weekend of the season, so I was always around fishing, even from being a baby – although I probably only fished in the real sense from about six years old. In those days, my father didn't have a car and I can vividly remember being ferried around from water to water via a tandem and sidecar – something you rarely see these days: most of my early fishing was wherever my father went. The early part of the season it would be on local lakes for tench, carp and bream. As the season progressed, chub and roach, with the odd barbel session included, and normally the winters would consist mainly of pike fishing.

I was born in Southall and lived in the Middlesex area for much of my youth. My father worked in Ealing as an instrument maker for a company called W. Ottway, which was just along the road from the split cane rod builders, B. James & Son. This is where a whole range of specialist rods were made, including the Richard Walker Mark IV rods, and naturally my father, being an angler, got to know the employees at B. James very well. So much so that he would help them out by machining the odd bits and pieces for them.

Of course, the favour was always returned in the way of fishing tackle so even when I was knee high to a grasshopper I had some of the latest rods available. I was even presented with prototypes of rods like the Kennet Perfection and the Avocet; so even from early on, tackle was never a problem.

My father didn't really specialise with one particular species of fish. He really just sought out the largest in any particular water. If he had any forte at all it was probably for tench. I do know that even during the fifties he came very close to record fish on more than one occasion. He still fishes today, but nowhere near as much and certainly more for the enjoyment of being on the bank than the actual size of fish. He was a great influence on much of my early fishing, and watching him approaching a water in his very stealthy manner still remains at the forefront of my mind even today.

We take a great many things for granted and believe we are all so clever with some of the latest rigs that are currently being developed. Many will not realise that this sort of thing has been going on for years and some of the dodges that were being employed in the fifties were, in some ways, more innovative than anything we do today.

I'll always remember one situation which brings a smile to my face. My father was trying to catch some very large roach that occupied a section of an old, disused canal. These were 2lb plus fish. The method was to fish breadcake right in the margins at night. Torches were completely taboo and I don't remember any night floats being around at that time. My father considered that float presentation was the best method. He came up with quite a unique solution to the problem. He fished a fairly largish porcupine quill on which he impaled a butt end of a lit cigarette. He managed to roll his own cigarettes in such a way that they would gradually burn away over a period of a quarter of an hour or so, which was often just enough time for him to get a take. Not only did the butt end emit a weak glow as the float disappeared beneath the surface, but there would be a faint hissing sound, so could this have been the first night float with built in alarm sound? This was just one of the many madcap ideas that he came up with.

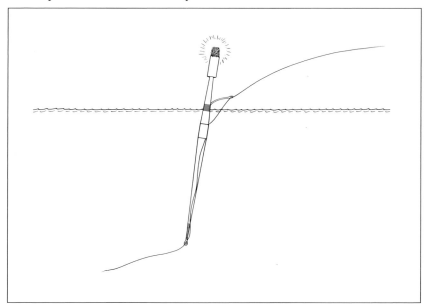

Dad's glowing float

Because my father was specialising in better quality fish, and generally the waters he was tackling at the time contained better than average specimens, a lot of this rubbed off on me and I was fortunate to catch some quite large chub, tench and bream when I was really very young. In some respects, I suppose I had an awful lot handed to me on a plate: in retrospect, I now realise that a lot of the learning curve had been cut short which, for me, was very nice. I do often wonder, however, what it would have been like if I'd had to do it on my own without my father's influence, because I do know that a lot of my school pals who were fishing at the time were only catching the odd small gudgeon and perch from the local canals. I really have his influence to be thankful for; I'm sure I would not have specialised in carp fishing as early as if I had just struggled along on my own. As well as my father having his marvellous contact with B. James, a little further down the road from the factory where he worked, was a fishing tackle shop run by Cliff Glenton. I doubt if many people will have heard of Cliff, but he was an excellent angler, especially where carp were concerned. He fished Savay long before the word got out and I believe I am right in saying that he was certainly one of the first to catch a 20 pounder there. Cliff Glenton also had a lot of dealings with and fished with Alex Renny, who ran that fabulous fishery, Wadhurst, in Sussex, famous for its wild carp. Whatever has happened to that water now, I wonder?

I don't actually remember catching my very first carp, as we caught quite a few small ones whilst fishing for other species. I do, however, remember catching my first double, which was in 1962 when I was 13 years old. This was from a gravel pit that was controlled by one of my local angling clubs near Hayes in Middlesex. This fish was caught on freelined floating bread crust and was one of quite a few that I caught during the summer of that year, although I was not completely specialising in carp at that time by any stretch of the imagination. It was more a case that I would go fishing for the weekend on a particular pit and fish for whatever looked catchable on the day, but again, trying to follow in my father's footsteps, rather than tiddler snatching on fine lines and small hooks, I would try to sort out the better fish, be it carp, tench, or bream. At that time, I did fish with a couple of my school pals at venues that were in cycling distance from home. My father still had no car so, save the odd trip by train, most of the fishing was done within a fifteen mile radius of home. My local venue was the nearby Osterley Park Lake which we fished in the evenings after school. At weekends we would usually go over to the pit near Hayes and occasionally visit some of the other Royal Parks ponds, but it was the Southall/Norwood angling club's pit at Hayes where we had the best chance of carp; many hours were spent there. The pit was probably about ten acres in size and the carp ran up to about mid doubles, but were mostly in the 5-10lb bracket. Certainly the number one method at the time was floating bread crust.

Without really knowing it, I was already starting to go my own way. I did still occasionally fish with my father but more often than not on my own, or with one particular school pal, Tommy Samson. I do remember though that when we were doing weekend stints he would often pop in to

Andy's first angling experience; his father

see if we were okay. In those days we would fish on upright seats with only a small umbrella for protection, and stop, when tired, to sleep in a tiny ridge tent which was pitched at the back of the swims. This was the way of things for a few years until we progressed to electric bite alarms and then we would sleep on a groundsheet next to the rods. You have to remember that everything had to be taken to the lake on our pushbikes so the items of tackle, sleeping and cooking equipment, were very limited.

Successful baits were a major problem. We had none of the modern day baits, so selective fishing was almost conducted at a stalking level only. I did use potatoes and bunches of worms, but these were nowhere near as productive as suspended crusts when the carp were not showing on the surface, and floating crusts when they were. At that time we had no experience of particle baits, not even sweetcorn. The first so called specialist bait that we got to hear about was luncheon meat; in fact we used Spam. This also accounted for quite a few carp.

My pal Tommy and I were really the only ones who fished for the carp at the Hayes pit. Any others caught there were generally by accident on float fished maggots. There were, however, a couple of people that I gleaned a lot of information from. Firstly, Cliff Glenton who was amidst

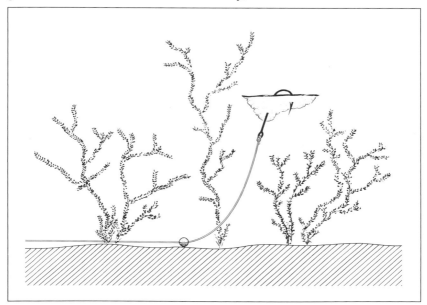

Suspended crust counterbalanced with a swan shot

the hierarchy in the carp fishing world, and although I am sure we were never let in on the latest info, the knowledge that he passed on was sound and very productive, and certainly made me think.

The other chap who had a great influence in those early days, was John Ruff. He worked with my father and, again, was an all round specimen hunter, but was slightly more biased to the carp side. John had caught some very good carp from venues I had never even heard of, and the one marvellous thing that he did have was transport; he owned an old Norton motorbike and would often take me, loaded to the gunnels, to new, distant venues. This was really my first contact outside my local biking area.

I had my first double at the age of 13 but I was no means a carp fishing specialist. I have never really gone out with the intention of specialising for carp. Even today I'm not really sure why I do it. There are so many branches of angling that I would love to spend time on; certainly, large barbel and big roach have a fascinating appeal for me. There just seems to be no contest; whenever I am getting ready to go fishing it's carp every time – very little else seems to enter my head. This is still very true today, I'm as keen now as ever, the difference being that there are so many other anglers carping; in my early teens I rarely bumped into another angler who was fishing for them. So who knows? Maybe in the next decade I may well be forced to change direction as the carping pressure becomes too intense, but life would certainly seem strange without carp. It seems to have slotted very nicely into my life and I have never, at any time, said to myself 'I'm going to be carp fishing for the next ten years before I move on to another species'. I love my carp fishing and still get that same excitement as another carp graces the net. They don't have to be monsters but, of course, it helps.

Going back to that first double all those years ago, I recollect how enormous that fish looked in comparison with its smaller brethren that we were used to catching. We caught a lot of carp in the 5-7lb bracket, but suddenly being confronted with a fish of 12lb plus, it looked enormous. I remember only too well that carp coming up to take the crust and as I hooked it, it turned and powered off down the pit. Although I had seen quite a few big fish being caught, especially by my father, left there with just Tommy for help, I was certainly nervous and, at one stage, panic stations set in. I remember Tommy chasing the carp around the margins with a net. We really must have looked a right couple of wallies, but somehow or other, more by luck than judgement, the fish was ours. It really must have been my day, as there was a chap a little further along the bank who had a camera with him – something we had just never owned – so I am glad to say I have a photograph of that first double.

At that time all the major influences on my fishing were at a local, rather than a national level. I rarely read any of the angling press of the time and was never part of any of the specimen groups in the area. In fact, there seemed to be very little outside of our small band that fished together, and I suppose we were so busy doing our own thing that we honestly didn't care. All my influence and information was very much at local level, first and foremost my father, and then Cliff Glenton and John Ruff.

Of course, odd whispers used to get back, as even then there was a grapevine, naturally. If I had any heroes of the day it had to be Jack Hilton, for his name would often crop up and naturally be associated with monsters. There was certainly some magical mystery surrounding his name, although I never, at the time, really knew what he caught or, in fact, where he was fishing. It would seem that he was a damn good angler and in some respects jogged my mind into thinking that perhaps there was more to it than I was experiencing in my local area.

I was, of course, now of an age where I was very much beginning to work things out for myself. I have a younger brother, Martin, who generally would now accompany my father. Although he never had the same enthusiasm as I did, he was a very good angler and at one stage held the junior chub record at 5lb 1oz., which, from memory, stood for a couple of seasons. He rarely fishes at all these days and never really got into it anything like my father and myself.

I can't remember there being one particular point in time when I made the decision to fish for carp to the exclusion of the other species. It was very much a summer occupation but I suppose, looking back, as the years went by more and more of the summer was taken up with carp fishing as the tench and bream took a back seat. The winters were certainly chub fishing on the Colne and Thames and piking at the local lakes and pits. Venues outside the local area would be those that John had chosen for himself, so I had little say about what we fished for on these trips.

It was on one such occasion, whilst fishing an area of the Upper Thames at Sandford, that we heard about a good carp venue called Marlborough Pool. We were asking this chap directions how to get there, and he said 'If you want to catch big carp I can show you a spot in one of the backwaters of the Thames near Sandford. Anyway, Marlborough Pool gets very busy and you might not like it'.

Anyway, so as not to look a gift horse in the mouth, we went to look for

these carp in the Thames and blimey, there were some real monsters –
well, they looked big to me at the time! In fact, I actually caught one that
day, a new personal best at 18lb. I think I would have been pleased with
it anywhere, but out of the Thames it was quite incredible. When you
think about it, the Thames isn't, even now, really carp fished so I was
quite chuffed with myself to catch this one. That was in 1965 and was to
remain my best carp for the next few seasons.

It was in 1969 that I caught my first 20 – an awful lot of fishing went on
between those years. What actually happened was that in 1969 I passed
my driving test and suddenly the world opened up to me. Not only could
I visit those places that John had taken me to, I could go in search of
carp venues that had only been whispers to me – Horton Kirby, Darenth
and Brooklands; by now I had really now got the bit between my teeth. I
started to join clubs in the Darenth valley but it was on my first session
at Brooklands lake, which I was fishing on a day ticket, that I caught my
first 20 pounder. In fact, that season I caught several twenties; the
strange thing was, they were caught on the same method as the Hayes pit
fish – floating bread crust, which was quite something really, because
there had been an awful lot of guys fishing Brooklands at the time. Jack
Hilton and Bill Quinlan had been there, and Gerry Savay and his

First experience of multiple catches at Brooklands lake

friends were fishing, but they were all using specialist baits. These were large balls of paste made up of secret ingredients, so to catch my first twenty on the old bread crust was very pleasing because at first I didn't think I stood a chance against these very experienced carp anglers. The nice thing was that very few of them were stalking fish or fishing on the surface, especially at any sort of range, for this was a method which we had really perfected at the Hayes pit.

I can't recall getting any special thrill from that first twenty. It was strange; it was an anti-climax slightly, as it really felt little different from catching the 18 pounder in 1965, although I must say I do rate that fish out of the Thames as one of my all time bests.

At Brooklands there were good doubles and low twenties caught quite regularly; this was certainly the most prolific water I had fished to date. Multiple catches around my local area were few and far between, but at Brooklands it was not unusual at all. That summer I caught five carp over 20lb and sixteen more over 10lb, so it was my best season to date. The knowledge that I gleaned from that water and the people who fished there helped me to realise just what it was capable of doing, given the right set of circumstances. Because I was catching fish as well, be it that they were on very standard baits, other anglers there started to talk to me and I was now hearing about Cat Food Specials and baits containing P. Y. M. (Phillips Yeast Mixture). This was a whole new world – although I remember getting kicked out of the kitchen when I started mixing up cans of Kit-e-Kat with groundbait.

I recall fishing a couple of other waters at about the time that I started fishing in Kent. The first was Southwold Park near Brentwood in Essex. I was very fortunate that one of my relations, an uncle in fact, lived in Brentwood, and occasionally I had my holidays there. The lake was only a short distance from his house and there was a very good head of carp in there, lots of singles, to about mid doubles.

Although I could only fish this place a couple of times a year, it was a prolific water and one that I was able to get to grips with. Baits were still very basic, bread in one shape or form, luncheon meat, and small potatoes. I had quite a few singles and a couple of doubles on most trips. In fact, I remember catching seven carp in a day from there, which was quite something; not huge fish, ranging between 3 and 10lb, but very exciting fishing, using fairly basic type tactics. This was one of the first venues where a good percentage of the fish population were carp, so naturally things were that much easier. Another venue that was buzzing at the time, was on the River Thames at Canbury Gardens, near Kingston. There was a hot water outlet that ran into the Thames from the power station. The nice thing was, I was able to get a train to Kingston and fish there for a couple of nights at a time. Very little was caught there during daylight hours and lob worms and large bunches of maggots accounted for most of the fish. We did catch bream, roach and eels but also a lot of carp. These again were up to about mid doubles but, of course, although the power station has now been closed, those carp must still be around and, of course, much larger.

I am sure that today there are more 20lb plus carp in the Thames than in any other river in the country, save maybe only the Trent. I am sure there are some really big fish residents there, that would shock many people. I certainly would not be surprised to see it produce a 40 pounder. It's almost the final frontier of carping in this country and it's really only the problems associated with boating and running water that keeps most of the specialist carp anglers away from it today. Over the years I've had my fair share of Thames carp, but I really must make the effort and devote a couple of full seasons on it – the results could be staggering. It's not only the Thames; as I said before, the Trent has enormous potential but there are many other rivers with carp in, so these are venues to look towards for the future.

Southwold Park success

2 — King Kent
the Carping County

I've already mentioned the Kent waters, but I'd like to look at Kent, the people who fished there, the waters, and the carp, in some detail. There were all sorts of people fishing there at the time. You have to remember that there was quite a buzz around the Kent carping. It would seem that almost every puddle in Kent held a good head of carp and it was like a magnet, attracting people from all over the country! Although I was not aware of it at the time, even Rod Hutchinson was travelling down to fish the area – so, of course, it wasn't just the locals. There were keenie carp anglers from just about every part of the country, so it was a marvellous opportunity to chat to people with the same goal. Looking back, this seems extraordinary, but for so many years during my early days of carp fishing, I rarely met another angler who was fishing for them: now it almost seemed that every other angler in Kent was fishing for carp.

Today, of course, it has become quite remarkable, with so many anglers specialising in carp – it is very difficult to get away from them, even on some of the most obscure waters in the country.

One bunch of lads fishing at Brooklands, who I became friendly with, made a lasting impression on me; so much so, that even today we still keep in contact. There was a group of about six of them who fished together. They were all a little younger than me and, quite honestly, at first looked like a bunch of dropouts. Hair down to their shoulders and wandering around in tanksuits, they looked a right weird bunch. How deceptive looks can be, for a greater bunch of guys you could not wish to meet – and very intelligent with it too. To look at them at first you would have thought that if they had a brain between them they would have been dangerous, but as it turned out they were to become scientists, photographers and biologists – it just goes to show! Amongst them were Paul Gummer, Bill Young and little Dickie Caldwell. The difference between these lads and the others, was their approach to the water. The big hype at the time was these new specialist paste baits, but Dickie and his band were very much into particle fishing, and extremely proficient as well. I think the reason for this was twofold. Firstly, as college lads they certainly didn't have the money to spend on specialist ingredients to make up paste baits, so particle fishing was a cheap alternative. Also, they were firm believers in margin fishing and capitalising on some of the more obscure corners of the lake that were overlooked by the other anglers. Here they could present their particle baits very proficiently. At the time their main baits were Black Eyed Beans and Maple Peas. These they used in quite large quantities, generally taking most of their fish at night when they moved into the quiet margins and little bays. They had some quite remarkable multiple catches – I remember Dickie taking a bag of seven fish in one short night session. Mostly they seemed to use the particles as they were, just soaking them overnight and boiling them up on the bank. It wasn't until later that they started adding flavours to them. Flavouring was mainly in the form of tinned soup, the particles being cooked in oxtail and tomato flavours. This was something of a revolution and they progressed to do very well with this approach in many of the Kent waters.

For myself, I tried not to have just a single approach to my fishing, but certainly had flirtations both with particles and with the specialist pastes. Together with the stalking, that I had learnt so well from my early carping, I could be very adaptable, whatever circumstances confronted me. It's nice that you can learn a little bit from your friends who have different approaches to the same species, and end up with a wealth of knowledge with which to attack the carp.

Out of this little group of anglers, it was probably Paul Gummer whom I became most friendly with, for as well as the carping, we also shared an interest in music and our favourite group was Pink Floyd, which was looked on by some as a strange following. I think Paul had just about every single record they had ever made and went to see them 'live' whenever he could. Kent got hold of me to such an extent that I eventually moved to the area. At the time it seemed to be the place to be, with so many carp waters in such a small area and the fishing got better and better.

The numbers of fish on the bank were certainly growing, and the general size was improving. During the 1970-71 season I managed to catch thirty one carp over 10lb., four of which were over 20lb. The 1972-73 season was really quite staggering and although, that season, I didn't catch a 20, I had seventy one doubles up to 19lb 12oz. Of course, I was hearing about new waters all the time, so the chances of expanding the potential for good catches was really at an all time high. It seemed that every water I went to, I would meet another angler who would tell me about yet another water in the area and I fished all sorts of places. Eventually, I ended up at Johnsons, which was the first time I had encountered a water with real monsters in for, even then, there was talk of thirty pounders. Johnsons was more like a mini complex within itself; there were three main lakes and I fished them all. The Railway Lake, the Island Lake and the Boat Lake, or at least, that's what they called them at the time – they've probably got different names now.

Out of the three, it was the Railway Lake that I liked fishing the most, probably because it was the least popular of the three and for most of the time you could have it to yourself. The Boat Lake was, undoubtedly, the most popular in the complex around that period. It appeared to have more carp in it than the rest, and also some very big tench. Here too, were many famous anglers, for I bumped into the likes of Len Burgess, Jim Gibbinson and Martin Gay.

There was also another chap around at the time whom I got to know very well, Terry Gage. He was a great guy, very single minded in his approach and quite a character. He fished with another Terry, Terry Davy. I think Terry Gage has probably put more time into Johnsons than anyone else who has fished there and, naturally, being a good angler, has caught many large carp; I'm sure he knows more about the water than anyone else. In fact, Terry is still fishing Johnsons even today.

A very young looking Johnsons Lake in the early 70's

Talking about famous people, I bumped into that gentle giant of carp angling, Fred Wilton, whilst fishing next door to Johnsons on the Leisure Sport Lake (Larkfield). He is surely one of the great characters in carp angling. I can remember watching him using one of his specialist protein floater baits at Larkfield, just slowly moving from swim to swim with a bag of baits, rod and reel, taking fish from here and there. Although they were obviously good doubles, he did not bother to photograph them – just enjoying himself really. It was fascinating to watch.

Each lake on the Johnsons complex was different in many ways. The Railway, my favourite, was fairly lightly stocked, with a few doubles, twenties and at least one thirty. Now this was quite different to what I had been used to at Brooklands and Horton Kirby and the like, for at these places there were stacks of fish; so Johnsons was completely different – with carp nowhere near as thick on the ground, but generally of a better size. Although I was determined to come to terms with the Railway Lake, I struggled there for quite some time and when I did start to get it right, the catches were by no means staggering. I remember quietly smiling to myself and thinking that I had done well when I caught three fish in the first month of the season. This is when I first met Rod Hutchinson. He had travelled down south to fish the Railway and had set up in the corner of the car park. I recall watching him, wading about up to his armpits in the water, cleaning a patch in the weed to put his baits down. That night he piled in a load of particles and proceeded to catch three twenties. He achieved in one night what had taken me a month, which really took the wind out of my sails. At the same time it opened my eyes; although I was also fishing on particles, I had only been using a few pounds at a time. I hate to think how many pounds Rod put in that night, but it certainly had the desired effect.

Particle baits were still fairly basic compared to some of the exotic varieties in use in more recent years. I suppose really we all take it for granted now, but at the time we kept these baits very much close to our chests. Sweetcorn, Black Eyes, Maples and Chick Peas were the baits we were using at the time. The sweetcorn would be used naturally and came from large catering cans; the Black Eyes and Chick Peas were boiled up in tomato soup and were absolutely brilliant baits; the Maples were again used on their own – left until they were a couple of days old, when fermentation started to take place. Even to this day, I have not found any flavour that increases the effectiveness of Maples, they work so well on their own. Most of these particles were used with two or three grains at a time on the hook. The modern carp man will think the tackle was pretty basic too. We had been using glass rods for a few seasons. These were generally a pound and a half test curve, two piece, ten or eleven feet in length. I could have been using rods made up from either Sportex or Conoflex blanks. Reels, I would probably have just changed over from the Intrepid Elite to Mitchell 300. The other reel around at this time, still being used by some carp anglers, was the Felton Crosswind. We had very little choice for hooks. I would generally use the Richard Walker Carp Hooks for snag free fishing or Low Water Salmons, cut off and solder blobbed, for heavier work. It also had to be around this time that the French Au Lion d'Or hooks first became available, and I used these for many seasons with great effect.

Mainlines would have been either Platil or Sylcast. Rigs were generally very simple. A small running lead stopped on the mainline with some sort of leger stop, or even just a two or three swan shot link leger stopped in the same manner.

Most of my fishing, up until now, had been done at very close range, so there was no need for really specialised tackle. I was using modified Heron bite indicators with long leads and a sounder box. I remember how much effort I took to camouflage everything. The rods would have to be matt finished, the reels were even dulled off and rod rests, buzzers,

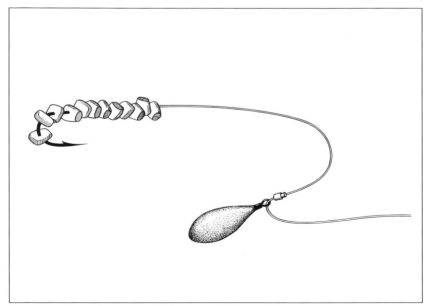

A great necklace of sweetcorn. 'What was I thinking of?'

and everything else were painted in camouflage colours. Isn't it a world apart from today, with our designer tee shirts, highly polished stainless steel rod rests, buzzer bars etc. With glossy finished rods, I certainly feel that some of the romance has gone out of carp fishing.

I've always been a bit of a loner when it comes to carping; I don't like being restricted. I like to go and do my own thing, when it suits me. I suppose, in some ways, it's selfish, but that's the way I am. I do admire people like Pete Springate and Kenny Hodder who seemed to have fished together for years. They have a certain rapport and it seems to work well for them. I have just never found any one person that I could spend that much time with.

Yes, I have fished alongside a lot of people, but it's not really true to say I have fished *with* them. I'm the sort of person who may well be sitting on one water and then decide I want to travel a hundred miles to go and fish another. I have these inclinations every now and then to just go and do it. I'm sure if I had a fishing partner he would not want to bow down to my every whim and, therefore, the flexibility that I have by fishing on my own would undoubtedly suffer.

That's probably the main reason, but the other is that I don't mind fishing on my own; I don't feel any particular need for company. Sure, it's nice to have someone to chat to, but I'm definitely happier – and fish better – on my own.

I fished a a great many waters during this period, some where I was successful and others where I failed. There were one or two that I would like to have spent more time at, but for one reason or another, I didn't. One of them was a ballast pit, which Terry Gage put me on to, which was run by the Tunbridge Wells Club. This was a prolific doubles water and in actual fact, this is where some of my best early winter carp fishing was done. Although I had caught carp in the winter before, I was now virtually fishing for them all the year round. The first winter carp I caught was probably at Osterley Park in the winter of 1967, but this was not by intention. I think I was fishing for livebait at the time. The first winter fish I caught by design, as it were, was at Brooklands – again, this was taken on a piece of suspended crust. I started the session fishing for pike, but as soon as I saw a carp swirl in the swim it did not take me long to change over and out went a piece of crust anchored about six inches off the bottom. The fish literally took within minutes of casting and was soon on the bank. I think this was probably the turning point, when I decided I would actually set out to fish for carp throughout the winter.

Going back to the Ballast Pits, I'll never forget a few sessions down there. It was one of those waters where the carp spent much of their time on the surface. I don't know why, but even in winter they could be caught on top. I would say that as many as 90% of the fish that I caught there were on surface baits of one sort or another. Mainly on crusts, but some on P.Y.M. floating cake mixture.

In addition, I used to dunk the crusts and floating cake in all sorts of weird and wonderful concoctions. Milk, honey, jam – anything to try and make them a little bit different. It really was a prolific water; very few singles, just lots and lots of doubles, up to about 20lb. I had some super days there and I can remember catching ten fish in a single day session. The water there fluctuated, as it was very close to the River Medway and this was during a particularly hot period of time, with low water. It was very weedy and most of the carp were lying just under the surface in the weed beds. I recall arriving around mid morning to the sight of fish all over the place. I set up three rods and cast the crusts on top of the weed. The middle rod took off – I remember it vividly. Almost at the same time, one of the others went, so I whacked into it, put that rod down and continued playing the first fish. I had just about heaved the first one out of the weed and into the net, when the third one went off. I couldn't believe it – I landed all three! Good doubles at that; tremendous fishing and, as I said, I went on to take ten fish that day.

I remember passing this water on to Paul Gummer and he fished there with a couple of his pals and they really took the place apart, even catching fish on the surface, at night, in the middle of a snowstorm – it was that sort of place.

This was a very interesting period. There had been a drastic drop in the water level at most of the pits within the Darenth Valley and it was a real opportunity to look round and map out all the various features, most of which were now exposed. This was quite an eye opener, for what we perceive looking from above the surface, is all so different once you have removed the water. Chasing round these waters and mapping them out was to hold me in good stead for many years.

Brooklands, although very low, did not really seem to suffer, but there was quite a problem at Horton Kirby. So much so, that it was closed to fishing and some of the carp were transferred, which I'm sure saved their lives. With so much of the water gone from Brooklands, the concentration of fish in certain areas was at an all time high and fortunately I was able to capitalise on this.

Without doubt, this was the best year for doubles to date; in that particular season I actually caught eighty four doubles, nine of which were over twenty. That really was my best season for carp – one of the milestones in my angling career.

Paul Gummer and the gang were still around; the water still had a great deal of attraction for them as well. I'm pretty sure it was that year when Paul caught his first twenty. He had taken loads and loads of doubles up to about 19½lbs and eventually got his just rewards.

There was also a lad that I semi-teamed up with, Steve Browne. He was a real up and coming keenie at the time, but I think, like so many, he eventually burnt himself out. I believe he doesn't even fish these days.

It was in the 1977-78 season that I caught my second thirty. This was from Johnsons; at long last, after quite a struggle, I felt I was really getting to grips with the place. Observing people like Rod Hutchinson and Terry Gage fishing there, combined with my own thoughts, I felt that at long last things were heading in the right direction and this particular fish, quite a well known leather, was the one I was really after. It was slightly down on its previous weight but at 33lb I certainly wasn't complaining. Again, it was the old Black Eyes that were the killing bait, flavoured in tomato soup.

It was strange, for after that, things at Railway Lake started to slip away for me and I struggled on for the rest of the year and, to be honest, caught very few fish. The Railway Lake did not give up its residents that easily; there were long periods of inactivity, save for the odd suicidal tench.

One interesting point about this thirty. It was the second fish that I had caught using a new hook link material. It was Paul Gummer who first got us thinking about using soft hook links, although I must admit I seemed to have had a mental block for quite a number of years, because my father always advocated using a braided terylene material, even back in the fifties. I always remember him having a spool of Green Butterfly braided terylene – or something similar to that!

Anyway, Paul certainly got us thinking again and, to try to get away from the stiff monofilaments, we started using the soft silk threads, the type they use for embroidery. This was really great stuff as it came in a multitude of colours, which you could select to blend in with the character of the swim. A problem was that it was all around the same breaking strain – from memory, about 12lb I believe, but this suited most of our fishing requirements anyway. It was a bit of a shock, thinking we had really come up with something fairly revolutionary to fool the carp, when I started to fail miserably at Railway. Then, that's carping isn't it? There are no guarantees.

There were several seasons between my first and second thirty and really, other than these two fish, I'm not sure that there were any other carp of this calibre in the waters where I was fishing. For most of the time, I was fishing waters where there were no thirties at all. It was a matter of keep going back to the ones where I knew they definitely existed and eventually winkle one out. This was a very exciting time, for now there was a growing following within the carp ranks and there was quite a lot of bankside discussion concerning methods, rigs and baits. Baits were now becoming far more sophisticated. Fred Wilton's theories on protein baits had started to leak out and, naturally, because of the spectacular results that Fred and his band of followers had achieved, everyone was itching to unlock the secrets of the protein bait theory. This was quite a revolution on the bait front and I personally feel that Fred has never been credited extensively enough with his unique, forward thinking. The particles scene had opened up many doors for me and through the seventies had contributed to a large percentage of the fish I put on the bank. There was too, a lot of hype on the particle front, with many lads talking about, and using mini particles – things like Rape Seed, Dari Seed, Buckwheat and Hemp. Tackle was being developed at a rate of knots. New specialist fast taper blanks were becoming available for long range casting and fishing lakes successfully

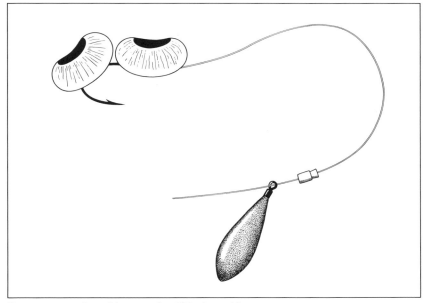

Better presentation with a couple of black eyed beans

at distance and became a new weapon in the carp angler's growing armoury. The other nice thing was that you could be so selective in your approach. With all these new found baits, we rarely had trouble with any other fish coming along and taking them. You could stick out a pile of Black Eyes and there they would stay until a carp came trundling along. The tench never used to take them and, believe it or not, there was a period when we were extensively using sweetcorn where this, too, never attracted the bream and tench.

It just goes to show how quickly the carp capitalised on a new food source and how much slower other species do so. Today, there are few waters where even tiger nuts can keep the hordes of tench and bream at bay, so I suppose, in some respects, the seventies had more to offer to the up and coming carp angler than any other period.

It wasn't only on the bait and rig front of course, it was the waters themselves. There seemed to have been an explosion of good carp stocking almost throughout the southern part of the country so there were now far more carp to fish for. In 1977 I joined the Carp Anglers' Association and also started writing about some of my exploits, although previously I had no inclination at all to join specialist organisations or do any writing. I'm not even sure how it came about.

I joined the C.A.A. because a friend had recommended it and this was the first specialist organisation that I had joined and frankly, I had never heard of them much before this time. I was far too intent on fishing for carp, looking for new waters and seeking out baits and it never dawned on me that there could be a social side to the sport. Carp fishing was everything to me, almost to the exclusion of everything else. My social life was also non existent. For most of the seventies and into the early eighties I lived for carp fishing, and really put it above and beyond everything else. Although I had a good managerial job, I'm sure if I had knuckled down a little bit harder I could really have done very well. I don't regret it though and I managed to live through it. Fortunately, I eventually saw the error of my ways. It was a very dangerous situation that I was getting myself into and I'm happy to say that I managed to come out of it the other side without too many scars. When I go carp fishing now, it is just for enjoyment; it is not a necessity; it has now become secondary and not the most important thing in my life. I don't think it would have made any difference whether I was successful or not. There were years when I caught very few fish and there must have been times when I asked myself what the hell was I doing it for? Sitting weekend after weekend, indicators never moving. I had some very hard years; it wasn't always easy and successful. I think we all go through a period like this in life – well, I certainly did. But still I went – it became almost like a drug, I just had to go carp fishing; every spare moment, weekends, evenings, holidays and all.

Eventually, of course, that nagging question arises in your mind, 'What on earth am I doing?' and starts to become more than a question. There's got to be more to life than this and, of course, there is. There is a lot more out there, a whole social world that I had forgotten existed. This didn't mean that I was about to give up my carp fishing, but get everything into perspective.

When I look back at that period, I'm sure I must have been very close to the edge. I'm not sure that I even realised there was an outside world. I never read a paper, watched TV or listened to a radio. I just went carp fishing. Very often there were times when, other than going to work, I really didn't know what day of the week it was. I was not alone in this, I know lots of people who have gone through exactly the same. Some have fallen by the wayside and packed in carp fishing altogether – it just got too much for them. Some don't even fish at all any more, never mind carp fishing. Some have even gone over the edge completely, mentally incapable of coping with life; the signs were there, but they never saw them. For the rest of us, you suddenly realise, okay, I've caught a lot of fish and perhaps it's time to sit back. Enough is enough. It's only a sport, a very enjoyable sport I grant you, but not to the exclusion of everything else. Somewhere along the way I reached that point and since then I've enjoyed my carp fishing.

3 — Surrey Exploits
First 30

Leaving Kent for a moment, another lake I've got fond memories of is Furnace Pond, a lovely little water in Sussex. We heard that it had recently had a large injection of large, fast growing Belgian fish, the same strain that were put into Duncan Kay's water. Unfortunately, however, those in Furnace did not survive.

Nevertheless, I had joined the water, so in order not to waste the ticket, I thought I would have a go. Now Furnace was another of those waters that supposedly had a mountain of large fish that always seemed to be caught when no one was around, or when no camera or scales were handy. Strange, isn't it?

Even at the time, I believe the water was vastly overstocked, so just what would have happened to the Belgian strain, had they survived, I hate to think. I enjoyed my time there, catching vast numbers of singles and doubles on the particle baits again. We were catching so many fish the locals were absolutely astounded that we hadn't caught any real whackers, for everyone knew that they were in there – apart from the carp themselves. There was one fish that did go just over twenty and I caught that a couple of times.

The locals said there were fish up to mid thirties, real monsters. In all fairness, they did have pictures of very large fish being stocked there, but I'm sure that they all died and, to be honest, I don't think there are any big ones left there now. The largest was probably that low twenty and I wouldn't be surprised if it's still the same today.

I fished there quite a lot the season I joined. It was very intense fishing with the thought that there might be one of these big fish still lurking around. I'd probably spent as much as four or five months fishing weekends and evenings and even did a few sessions during the winter. I still did not catch any of the big ones, nor ever saw them – although it was not a particularly good water for studying fish; it was always quite dirty, so unless the fish were on the surface, they were difficult to observe.

I fished Furnace Lake with a local angler from Carshalton called Malcolm. He had only been carping for a couple of seasons but was indeed a very keen and enthusiastic angler. As he had no transport, it was fairly convenient for me to pick him up on my way to the lake, usually on a Friday night, for a weekend session. I too, was glad of the company. At least now some of the time consuming bait preparation could be shared.

Furnace certainly responded to the particle treatment and although we used almost everything from Dari seeds to kidney beans, by far the bulk of the fish were caught on flavoured chick peas. These we would purchase in 50 kilo sacks to get the best price , then large buckets, probably containing 5 kilos or so of dry weight chicks were soaked overnight. We always added flavour and colour, usually red or orange, with strawberry or banana flavouring. The chicks were then boiled for about half an hour to make them fairly soft. We used an enormous amount of bait most weekends throughout the summer and, between the two of us, we would often come away with thirty or more fish during that time. These were mainly high singles and low doubles with the occasional mid double if we were lucky. The fishing was done at close range, no more than about fifteen yards out from the bank. We both used three rods – I was on my 11ft Cloopers and ABU Cardinal 66 Expresses. Rods would be set high, Kent style, some 3ft off the ground and Fairy Liquid

A perfect Furnace linear

bottle tops hung between the butt and the second ring with long drops, the bottle tops almost touching the ground.

Rigs were very simple, seven or eight pound line straight through to a size 6 Jack Hilton hook on which two Chick Peas were impaled, leaving most of the bend and point exposed. A three quarter ounce free running Arlesey Bomb was stopped about nine inches from the hook with a little plastic leger stop.

Several catapult loads of Chicks would be dispensed in the swim and then the hook bait cast among them. We virtually always got pre-emptive line bites and twitches which would have us hovering over the rods. This would then be followed several minutes later by the Fairy Liquid bottle top sailing into the ring and the reel churning furiously if you could not get your hands to the rod in time. Very often, a shoal of carp would come into the swim and it was by no means unusual to have to contend with two takes at the same time.

The carp at Furnace also responded well to floater tactics when the weather was hot and muggy, especially if there was any sort of ripple on the lake. This was a time when I was using Specialist Floating Cakes. I would mix up ten ounce lots of milk powders, usually casein, lac-talbumin and calcium caseinate; a little gluten as a binder and a teas-poon of baking powder to make the mixture rise. All the powders were mixed up with a dozen large eggs and cooked in the oven in a large bak-ing tin for a couple of hours. You ended up with a really tough piece of floating cake with lots of good, crusty edges to keep away the attentions of any nuisance fish. Although we did flavour the cakes from time to time, I can honestly say that at Furnace it didn't seem to make that much difference.

Oh, and of course, I must not forget the horrendous eel problems that we encountered at the lake. It was one of the reasons that we used par-ticles, because paste baits were absolutely devastated by these little bootlace size creatures that seemed to have a never ending appetite for the angler's baits! At times the problem was so bad that we would even catch them on surface baits, something that I have never come across anywhere else.

I also had a flirtation with amino acids in paste baits. I had read some-where that it may be possible to get round the eels with varying com-binations of aminos. I used them in combination with quite a soft paste bait, containing various combinations of glutamic, aspartic, tyrosine, glycine, alanine, isoleusine and lysine. Talk about get yourself confused! I had again fallen into the trap of trying to create the ultimate bait. Many hours were spent reading up on every available organic chemistry book, plus all the relative papers I could lay my hands on and what did it all end in? One big headache, for it's certainly a science that I couldn't get my head round and relate it to carp fishing. I ended up with a very expensive bait that the eels obviously thought was the best thing since sliced bread, so it was back to chick peas.

The other bait that we occasionally used at Furnace was par boiled potatoes. This did have the habit of sorting out one or two better fish but probably more important to us at the time was the fact that it was a good bait to use at night to combat the ever present eels and to get a good night's kip, for when you did get a take on the potatoes, they rarely stopped giving you enough time to emerge from the sleeping bag, get to the rods and strike.

I did fish there for a short time in the second season, mainly because it was such a lovely looking water, with a nice atmosphere, and I met and made some good friends there also. There was Bob Baker, Albert Romp – another famous fishing duo; also a lad who was to become a good friend of mine, John Downes who, tragically, was killed in a road accident a few years ago. This was a very sad loss to the carp world and John was one of the few people who really made me laugh.

There was also Disco Martin, who nearly killed someone there with a hard boiled egg. There was a bit of an eel problem at Furnace and to try to get over it, Martin tried to use a hard boiled egg as bait, but cracked off on the cast and knocked out a guy fishing out on the dam wall, when the egg hit him squarely on the forehead.

Furnace was very close to the grounds of a monastery and, naturally, there were many stories of strange happenings that took place there – many of which were plausible, as the monks used to wander around the lakes under a vow of silence and would often appear, as if by magic, at the back of the swim observing the anglers: very eerie stuff, but it all went to make up the character of the lake.

My first thirty was caught at a place called Coolgreena in deepest Surrey. I had visited this pit several times, as it was a place we had seen advertised in the angling press and it was somewhere that my old mate, Johnny Ruff, had taken me to several times, before I passed my driving test. That was in 1974 and the fish weighed 30lb 4oz. A colossal fish to me at the time.

This particular carp probably made the most impression on me ever. Not because it was a very good looking fish or anything, but it was so much bigger than anything else I had ever caught. At Brooklands and Kirby I had only caught them to low twenties, and at Johnsons up to mid twenties, so this was 5lb bigger than anything I had ever landed before. I had caught it on floating breadcrust at the second proper attempt of fishing the water specifically for carp. I still have fond memories of that fish, and it is one that, until recently, has been around for some time and has been many people's personal best.

Coolgreena was part of a complex of three pits at Send in Surrey. Two of the pits, Sandersons and Langhams, were run by the Woking Club and they eventually took over Coolgreena and renamed it Cobbetts. In fact, it's my old mate, the head bailiff of the Woking Club, Ron Buss, who caught the fish several times, and somewhere along the way it was nicknamed 'Gertie Thirty'. Unfortunately, that fish is now dead and to Ron's credit, he paid to have it set up and it's now in residence over his mantelpiece. I have terrific memories of the place and I was to fish it again in the eighties.

Langhams double figure common which fell to a potato

The pits at Send were one of the cult waters of the sixties and seventies and, out of the three, it was Langhams that received most of the attention. Many of the names in carp angling at the time either fished there, or tried to fish there. The hierarchy who were running the water at the time were obviously quite aware of the potential at Langhams and tried to keep away any outsiders. Both Hilton and Quinlan were among the many famous anglers who wet their lines there and even my old mate, Chris Ball, attempted it but fell foul of the hierarchy. Undoubtedly, the king pin on the pits was local angler, Johnny Brough, who fished everyone out of sight. He was certainly one of the unsung heroes of the sport; he held the Surrey record for quite a few years with a 33½lb mirror which he caught from the water in 1966 and which was then a monster anywhere, let alone in the Surrey area. As the years went on, attitudes did change at Send, but it will never ever be a free for all. Meticulous vetting of would be anglers will always ensure that a degree of sanity still remains on those prestigious pits.

4 — The Way is Clear

Most of the waters that I have fished over the years were known to me as carp waters before I fished them. I would obviously go and look around first, to see if I could actually see fish for myself. You often read that you should go and seek out every piece of blue on your local Ordnance Survey map with the hope of finding another Redmire, or at least a bit of water with some unknown carp in. Great in theory, but invariably it doesn't work these days.

Of course, this was the way a lot of the early pioneers sorted out their waters, but I don't class myself in that category. I don't think I can ever claim to have found a new water anywhere! Usually it is the case that all the ones that I have fished have been known by other anglers and the information has been passed round the grapevine. Of course, I will always try and ensure that I sort out the facts from the sheer romancing, for it would seem that every single water, up and down the country, has a 30lb common carp in it that has never been caught. Naturally there is much speculation and wishful thinking within the ranks of angling, although I should say here and now that I too have fallen foul of this syndrome. I had a chance meeting with an angler by the name of Mike Oyez, who had done quite a bit of writing in the B.C.S.G. magazines, and I was a fan of his penwork. Now this guy could certainly tell a story – many of which were based around some of the many monster carp that he had either caught or seen. Mike ran his own little syndicate water called Wytchwood (Stockley Road), consisting of two small gravel pits near Colnebrook, adjacent to Heathrow Airport. After our initial meeting which, from memory, was at the Crooked Billet at Staines, at one of the B.C.S.G. regional meetings, I arranged to pop round to his house for a further chat, with the idea in the back of my mind that I could persuade him to let me have a place on his syndicate. I remember that second meeting very well. We sat in his little study at his home in Hayes and really, he just talked. I sat there open mouthed, listening to all these wonderful stories and my sensibilities and grasp on reality suddenly left me. I was hooked! Old Mike could really tell a story – I'm sure he missed out on his true vocation. I believed his stories and, because of his close relationship with the likes of Walker and Mohan, they were bound to have some credibility. Looking back, I believe that Mike was sincere about the tales himself, as he's a real Mills and Boon romantic.

After several more meetings I was granted a place on the syndicate. This meant more meetings in that marvellous little study where, at the time, was housed the rod that Richard Walker caught the record carp on, and the inscribed Mitchell 300 from the Walker v Sales match, as well as many other marvellous old paintings, rods, etc.

On the very first trip to the waters, I met a very good angler called John Richards. He was a really smashing guy and we teamed up together and attacked the water and by heck, did we catch a lot of fish. We had loads and loads of singles and doubles and the odd twenty pounder but no monsters. In fact, no monsters were ever hooked; come to that, no monsters were ever seen and, in reality, I don't think there were ever any monsters in there, so I was really taken in.

This was such an experience that it has really made me pessimistic on virtually every water I have fished since. The only time you can be absolutely sure about the monsters is when they are in the bottom of your landing net.

The Wytchwood experience was one that I would not have missed though. It was the first water where I had used small floating particles; these were of the pet food variety, the main two being Meow Mix and

Night time common from Mike's water

Felix Meaty Crunch. This type of fishing was a real revolution. We had heard whispers on the grapevine that they were even very successful at the extremely difficult Ashlea Pool. Those carp really loved them. The problem was that for most of the summer the carp in Mike's water were in the weed, and Mike put so many obstacles in your way there had to be a bit of rule bending to ensure that we caught a lot of fish. He used to cut out these swims he'd call Onions, which consisted of a thin channel cut out from the weed, terminating in a little pool about ten feet in diameter and of course, the carp avoided these like the plague. Another of his rules was that there was no sleeping whilst the baits were out and he would creep round in the middle of the night with his giant Alsatian – which I'm sure only fed on dozing carp anglers! He would steal up on you in the early hours of the morning and, with his face inches from yours, he'd say 'You're not asleep Little, are you?'

If that wasn't bad enough, there would be slippery poles to navigate to reach the prestigious island swims, or the vertical double ladder on which you certainly risked life and limb to climb down. Then there was Colditz and the Bunker, and all sorts of other swims that just seemed to form major obstacles to ensure that you could not fish comfortably. When he found out about the cat biscuits it was goodbye Andy and

Typical Wytchwood fish caught on particles

John, but, as I say, it was an experience not to be missed.

Many years later when William Boyers took the water back from Mike and it was drained down to extract the fish, there was, of course, nothing other than what we had actually caught there. I was really hoping in my heart of hearts that there would be an unseen monster there, because Mike had such an influence on me and I really did believe every word, but I was just hoodwinked. I suppose in some respects we need these characters to make up the carping world, but it was a hard lesson learned.

There are stacks of waters and new ones are coming up all the time. These generally aren't old, forgotten water with lunkers that have been there for years, they are more likely to be new waters, recently stocked with fast growing fish. In addition, there are plenty just waiting to be rediscovered.

Many of the doubles waters of the seventies will become the twenty and thirty waters of the eighties and nineties. Years elapse, the memory fades, and all of a sudden a 30lb carp turns up on a water that you had forgotten, which at the time only contained mediocre fish. This has certainly happened to me on a number of occasions. You can never tell; I have written off waters where the carp look like they had no chance of ever making any more than low twenties and suddenly, the environment has changed for one reason or another and the fish have put on many pounds in a relatively short space of time.

Of course, the majority of people will go to a known water, and I'm no different, but it doesn't stop you looking for new venues, hoping you are going to find that little piece of heaven. They are few and far between but, who knows, perhaps there are other Redmires out there just waiting to be discovered.

I always spend a lot of time mapping out any waters that I am about to fish, checking the depth, what the bottom is made up of and pinpointing the contours. Gravel pits have a real fascination for me.

On most of our southern pits there are just so many features; there are times when there are more small holding areas and feeding areas than we could possibly ever fish. I'm always staggered by the number of so called good carp anglers who are fishing in a swim and haven't a clue what is in front of them. They are only fishing there because Joe angler caught a fish from the spot last week. Very few would even know the depth of the water they were fishing in, let alone the topography of the swim. I'm always looking for small features that everyone else has missed; most anglers can find bars okay, but it's little depressions, a steeper drop off, a small shelf on a bar, that I'm always searching for.

Carp love to follow these features, especially when they are seeking out food. Any of these small depressions, or out of the ordinary features, will invariably hold food of some description. A small layer of silt will have built up and so the food chain begins; even on the plainest bottoms there will always be something out of the ordinary that will attract carp. Gravel pits are absolutely full of such places.

Natural lakes though, will be completely different in character and they too will hold their little secrets. For example, I will spend many hours checking the depth for silt and maybe try to find a small, sandy patch. Carp will often create their own depressions in the silty bottoms where they have been digging for bloodworms and small crustaceans. All of these features I will painstakingly map out, because although it will probably be possible to catch carp in lots of other areas, if I am to catch the lion's share of the fish, I need to work just that little bit harder.

To my way of thinking, location is everything. To state the obvious, there is very little point in spending hours behind a lovely set up, with the latest rigs and the best baits, if there are no carp in the swim. The old adage of six hours looking and one hour fishing when you have found them, still holds true today.

As well as mapping out the features, I take notice of compass direction as many of these little spots will be affected by wind direction and weather conditions, so even when I am at home I will probably have a good idea where to start looking for carp before I have seen the lake.

Weed beds hold another mystery and most anglers will avoid them, opting to fish the clearer parts of the lake, but, here too, will be an abundance of food and also cover for the carp. I will always try to form a mental picture of exactly what it looks like beneath the surface. Most rooted weed is little different from any other plant life; it starts off with a main stem and gradually fans out towards the top as it spreads out towards light and oxygen. Therefore, what from the surface would, at first, seem to be an impenetrable carpet of weed, underneath there will, in fact, be a lot of room for the carp to move around – almost like a massive network of motorways. Find the right route and you could stack up!

Blanket type weed and amphibious varieties of water plants again are worth investigating, because they will all hold food of some description which carp will forage for at various times.

I probably get as much pleasure out of unlocking the watery secrets of any venue as I do from catching carp from them. I suppose, in reality, it goes hand in hand. Once you have sorted out the wood from the trees, the way becomes very clear. You get to know what to look for and, providing your timing is right and the weather conditions allow, the carp won't be far away.

Going back to bait, things have progressed in leaps and bounds. The late seventies were an all time high for bait formulations. The Wilton theory had been well and truly exposed and whether you agreed with it or not, it couldn't be ignored, As well as the milk protein type baits, we had also discovered a cheaper version of a good, attractive bait, by using bird food and, on some waters, it was really producing the goods. Some of the early boilie mixes I would have been using at the time would be as follows:

2oz Yestamin
3oz Casein
1oz Lactalbumin (Yellow New Zealand)
1oz Casilan (Calcium Caseinate)
1oz Soya Isolate
2oz Protoveg (Textured Vegetable Protein)

3oz Nectarblend
3oz P.T.X.
2oz Casilan (Calcium Caseinate)
2oz Robin Red

3oz Casein
2oz Protoveg (Textured Vegetable Protein)
1oz Lactalbumin
1oz Casilan (Calcium Caseinate)
1oz Soya Isolate
1oz Wheat Gluten
1oz Sucron
10ml Maple Flavouring plus colour.

Although these were nothing particularly revolutionary at the time, they were very consistent catchers of carp.

I started to really get caught up on the bait roundabout and began to use amino acids, and was forever searching out new ingredients. Concentrated flavours were also becoming more readily available. The choice was becoming quite spectacular when you consider that five years before, a tin of Kit-E-Kat was about as exotic as we could get.

I fell into the same trap as many and far too much emphasis was being put on the bait; it was getting to quite a ridiculous state, even going to the extremes of matching various amino acids to the pH level of the water, and even changing the mix at various times during the day. At one stage, it all seemed to make a difference but now of course, with the benefit of hindsight, I know this is not true. There are good baits and there are slightly better baits, but there is no ultimate bait that will draw fish from every part of the lake and make a bad angler a successful one.

I'm glad to say that now bait has only become one tiny part of the jigsaw puzzle and nowhere near as much emphasis is placed on it; there are far too many more important things. There are people who almost make a hobby out of the bait making itself, and I would never knock them for doing so. My only concern is that the average Joe angler thinks it's a short cut to success which, of course, it is not.

5 — Progression

Most of my carping, up until the late seventies, had been done at short to medium range,but I joined Darenth, and on the big lake, mainly because of the extra pressure it was receiving, many of the fish spent much of their time away from the near margins and out among the islands, so this was now a whole new ball game. There were times when I was having to present bait at distances in excess of 80 yards.

First, the bait itself had to be modified. Generally I would only be boiling the bait for the minimum time, just to put a skin on it. But these fairly soft baits just would not catapult out, so the ingredients were changed slightly and we boiled them for longer. With a roughly three quarters of an inch diameter boilie, it was possible to catapult out the freebies in excess of 80 yards in the right conditions.

Rods too had changed. Fast taper, fibre glass blanks had just become available and I managed to get hold of some of the early Green 'Clooper' carp rods from Going Brothers of Southend. These rods were something of a revolution, being a very fast taper and 11 feet in length. I believe they were the brainchild of Jim Gibbinson and Martin Ashby. Up until now, the most commonly used rods were 10 feet, either compound or through action. The number of rings had also been cut down and I made mine up with eight on, including the tip. The 'Cloopers' matched up with my Mitchell 300's, with the spools overfilled with 8lb line. I now found that I could cast in excess of 100 yards, but unfortunately couldn't get the freebies that distance. Of course I was by now using much larger leger weights than ever before, for 2oz was needed to project the baits out at this distance.

The next thing to change was the way I mounted the baits. With the soft paste baits and skinned boilies, we just buried the hook inside the baits and when a take came, the hooks were struck out fairly easily, but with the harder, longer boiled baits, this proved to be impossible. I had some marvellous takes but could only manage to hook one in every ten, so something had to be done. At first I thought that as little of the hook should be showing as possible so I went from burying the hook in the baits to using a small size 10 just nicked through the skin of the boilies.

All of a sudden, the takes began to change. They became much faster and the conversion ratio was greater than it had ever been. It was like a whole new world opening up. As with the water craft and the bait syndrome, I suddenly found that I was on the threshold of a new understanding of bait presentation. At this point in time I thought there was just no stopping it.

The rigs were modified to such an extent that I ended up using size 2 fine wire Match Blues, which were a long shank spade end hook. At least 75% of the hook was now left hanging out of the bait and the hook links themselves were made quite short. At first it was more for tangle free casting, but as time went on, it became apparent that a hook link of about six inches in combination with these large hooks would give you almost 100% hooking ratio takes. The leger weight itself also went through something of a change. Generally, it would have been fished on a running link, anything between 2 inches and 12 inches. I now had the leger weight free running directly on the mainline. Although I was not aware of it at the time, this was probably one of the first self hooking bolt rigs being used.

The first season I was at Darenth, I spent most of my time on the big lake, mainly because it was completely different fishing to any I had

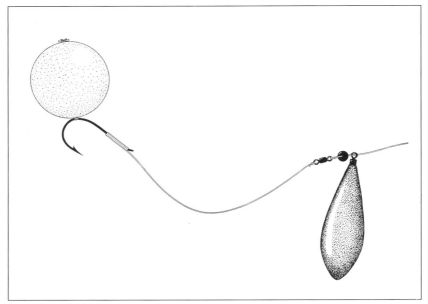

My original 'bolt' rig

done before. Generally, I would be fishing at long range and I became quite fascinated by this new concept. I really wanted to become very proficient at long range casting and accuracy in ground baiting at a distance.

During this era, the mid to late seventies, Darenth was becoming a very popular water, and I was to meet lots of other very good anglers with whom I became friends. There was Micky Sly, who was there on his first season, Lee Jackson and Alan Smith, two very proficient carp anglers, and Pete Amey, one of the bailiffs who was also a judo expert and quite a character with it. So prolific was the fishing at Darenth, on the big lake, that I stayed there right throughout the winter. In fact, the winter sessions were much more predictable, and certainly more productive, than those in the summer. What had actually happened is that I think ninety per cent of the carp had moved to one part of the lake. This was an area out in front of the first island and there were about six swims that you could fish to reach this particular spot – from either of the Willow swims, from the Middle Road Bank swims or the High Bank or Elderberries. In this area, just about in the centre of the lake and in front of the first island, there seemed to be a whole load of fish shoaled up. From memory, there was about fourteen feet of water and there was a very clean bottom; the other anglers present, and I, had some tremendous catches from this particular hot spot. The following season I decided to move on to the Tip Lake and the Finger Lake. Now this was more like being back on my old close range fishing with particles. In actual fact, on the Tip Lake, that's what I started off with, and it was to be the Mini Maples I used first.

I really fell in love with the Tip Lake and I would go as far as to say it is high on my list of all time favourites; there were some fabulous fish in there, to just under thirty pounds. At that time, there were probably as many as fifteen fish in excess of twenty five pounds, which was quite staggering. Because the stocking levels were nowhere near as high as on the big lake, and some of the swims were somewhat difficult to fish, there was always plenty of space to move around, so there were many stalking opportunities, which really suited my style of fishing.

The first few months of the season were very successful indeed – the Mini Maples taking the lion's share of the fish. I also had one or two on kidney beans, just fished over the top of the Mini Maples and also the odd one or two fish on strawberry flavoured Chick Peas.

By the beginning of September that year, most of the better fish had come out of the Tip Lake and I am pleased to say I had a fair few of them myself, including the one known as B.B., in excess of 29lb. I had been alternating between the Tip Lake and the Finger Lake, but doing more time on the Tip Lake. After September, I changed and spent more time on the Finger Lake. Here, I thought the particle approach would also work, but whether the particular particles I was using had been used previously, I don't know – but they failed miserably. It wasn't until I went back onto the boilies, indeed, very small boilies, that I started to get success. The bait that I was using was the Felix Meaty Crunch ground down and mixed with rice powder and gluten; this was a superb bait. I was rolling these out into long, thin ropes and cutting them up with a knife so I ended up with a small cylinder, roughly a quarter of an inch in diameter and just over a quarter of an inch long. This was mass baiting with mini boilies. I really started to bait up heavily along the bar that runs for three quarters of the length of the Finger Lake. There were several little depressions in this bar, where the carp used to congregate from time to time. It was pinpointing these depressions in the bar that enabled me to capitalise on the situation. Pounds of these chopped up boilies would be put in a very small area, critical baiting up. Often I would see the carp moving into the baited area long before I got a take and with several pounds of freebies around either of the hook baits, it was usually twenty minutes, or maybe half an hour, after the first signs of the carp's activity before I got a take.

The fish in the Finger Lake at that particular time had a very high average weight. I caught more over twenty than under twenty; there were several mid twenties and one or two upper twenties. I was very fortunate to catch the largest fish in the lake twice – this was a beautiful fish called 'Curlytail'. It had come out earlier in the season whilst I was fishing the Tip Lake, at 30lb 8oz. The first time I caught it, it was two or three ounces up on that, but the second time it was 31lb 10oz, so I was well pleased, for this was the new Finger Lake record.

However, there was one other fish that I really wanted to catch there, but it eluded me completely. This was the 'Pilgrim'. It was an ironic situation that occurred around this particular fish, for the next season I tried again for the 'Pilgrim', not knowing that it had been moved several weeks before I started, and it was now a resident in the Tip Lake. It wasn't until a lad came over and asked me to photograph a fish for him on the Tip Lake, that I realised exactly what had happened. For, as you have probably guessed, it was the 'Pilgrim' he had just caught! Talk about banging your head against a brick wall! I had no chance of catching it!

It was during that season that a band of very keen carpers, who were later to become famous, started to fish Darenth. They were Kevin Maddocks, Lennie Middleton, Keith Gillings and Bob Davis. Occasionally they would be joined by Paul Bray. Now this group of anglers certainly had active minds and tried all sorts of things when they initially started to fish at the big lake. It was obvious by their approach to the water that they were really going to do the business there. There were a few events that happened over the next few months that will stay in my mind forever. I suppose, in some respects, I was very fortunate that for most of the time I was fishing on my own and therefore seemed to be much more accepted into groups of other anglers, and this was certainly the case with Lennie Middleton, for we hit it off immediately and were to become very good friends. Although we shared a mutual admiration for carp, and carp fishing, there was still a slight air of secrecy about baits and rigs. It soon became obvious that Lennie and his band of friends were doing something a little different from the rest. Their takes were that much better, there were more of them, and they had a higher average of fish on the bank.

My own presentation, with most of the hook outside the bait, was also doing very well, which wasn't surprising when you consider that the great percentage of the anglers, certainly on the big lake, were still fishing with their rods quite high, hooks buried in the bait and fishing short

Curly Tail at 30.10 – a Finger Lake record

drops with Fairy Liquid bottle tops, still hitting twitches. By now, my takes were so fast I had to resort back to open bail arm fishing, even at long range; with the heavy leads, short hook links and much of the hook exposed, the takes were often blistering.

Something else that had happened by accident was that I was starting to clip up against the wind and it was very noticeable that every time there was a big wind on the lake and I had to clip up, the takes were that much faster, so I started to clip up, even in very calm conditions. It was quite amazing to watch the rod tip pull round several inches before the line came out of the clip, followed by a blistering take. Now Lennie and his lads, although they were fishing a different method to the one I was using, were still getting a lot of very good takes. Generally, they would fish with fairly slack lines with very light bobbins and the rods fairly low to the water, so they were obviously doing something to induce very confident takes, or some degree of self hooking. The more I got to know Lennie, the more obvious it became that they had some little secret. There were many times during the autumn of that year that Lennie got into conversation with me, regarding rigs and set ups. Although he would have liked to tell me, he was sworn to secrecy by the others which, as far as I was concerned, was fair enough. The set up they were using had quite intrigued me, because although both Lennie and Kevin were catching an awful lot of fish, they were striking at different times, which was fascinating. Lennie told me that it was agreed that on this new set up they were using, Kevin would strike as soon as he possibly could once the takes started, and Lennie would leave the take to develop for varying lengths of time. At one stage I believe he was letting the takes go for at least a minute before striking. Now, as you can imagine, on a lake which is normally known for twitcher hitting, to let a take go roaring off for a minute was quite something!

Certainly, I know Lennie had trouble curbing his impatience and there was one period when it became quite bizarre. He would use all sorts of tactics to slow his reactions down to stop him striking – from putting towels over the butts of his rod and reels to alert him to the fact that he had to wait to taking his reel handles off and burying them in the bottom of his tackle box. It was during early winter, whilst fishing with Lennie in the Willows Swim, that it all became very clear what they were up to and it was by pure chance that a situation occurred that made Lennie decide to tell me all.

I was still fishing with my short hook links – the large Match Blues, with most of it sticking out of the bait. The problem I was experiencing, however, was that on long range casting, especially in adverse conditions, baits would often be cast off. Because there was very little of the bait on the hook and I was making the baits harder to combat against the nuisance fish, they would easily fly off, so I had to look out for a new solution to overcome this problem. What I decided to do was to lash the boilie to the spade end of the hook with a short piece of nylon. Now this would generally be just four or five pounds breaking strain and tied directly to the spade, just below the whipping knot. There were times when there was probably no more than an eighth of an inch, certainly a quarter of an inch absolute maximum, of freeplay between the bait and the hook. Much of this depended on how cold my fingers were when tying them up!

Now this was the set up that I was using on that particular day when Lennie and I doubled up in the Willow Swim. On seeing me cast this rig out, he immediately said to me, 'Ah, you've guessed what we've been using'.

To be honest, I didn't know what he was talking about. It was then that Lennie started to tell me about the hair rig.

'The hair rig, what on earth is the hair rig?' I asked him.

This was apparently the name that Lennie and his friends had given to the set up they had been using for most of the season. This was the rig,

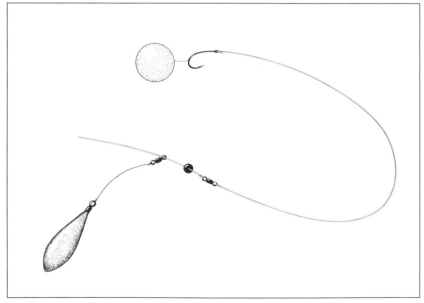

The famous hair rig

he explained, that had been conceived one evening while he and Kevin Maddocks were messing about in Kevin's fish tank. He had this idea that if he could divorce the bait from the hook in such a way that they were only linked by a very fine filament, the carp would gain confidence in taking bait that wasn't restricted by the hook. They assumed that most of the carp were actually picking up the bait lightly in their mouths before eventually taking it right the way back to their pharyngeal teeth. By divorcing one from the other by the fine filament, it would actually fool the carp into thinking there they were actually a separate entity, whereas, in fact, they were joined together.

It was on this particular evening that Lennie actually took a hair from his head, tied it on to the bend of a hook and then to a bait and tried the set up in Kevin's tank. The response from the carp was very exciting to say the least, he explained, and so the hair rig was born.

We talked long into the night about all sorts of different set ups and I can honestly say, over my many years of carp fishing and of all the people I have met in those years, Lennie Middleton is certainly the most forward thinking angler that I have ever had the pleasure to fish with. He went to such extremes as making a mocked up carp's head, including working mouth and gill covers, just to try to learn more about how these fish actually fed, and the reaction of different rigs when they were taken by the carp.

Of course, this was all very exciting and I asked him if I could also use a similar set up. As he thought I had already sussed out what he was doing, there was no problem at all. So it was this sheer coincidence that we were both drawn into this conversation; I had certainly not, by no stretch of the imagination, ever conceived that my rig was anywhere near a parallel to his own work.

The winter of '79 at Darenth was fantastic from the fishing point of view. The only problem that Lennie and I encountered was that we were only fishing on Friday and Saturday nights and going home on Sunday. For some reason or other, this is just when the lake appeared to keep freezing up. It would thaw out during the week, only to be frozen over again by Thursday evening, so this was very frustrating, to say the least, but when we could get baits in the water, we caught fish. I remember clearly that there were two or three occasions when we actually managed to cast out, only for the lake to freeze over! Sometimes, after it had, we would have a take and would have to play the carp back under the ice. A real performance, as you can imagine.

I carried on using my Felix Meaty Crunch boilies for some time and as the winter dragged on, I eventually changed over to some new Maple

Andy's ultra cult Darenth set-up, mid '70's

A side-hooked boilie makes its way out to the island. Note height of rods!

Kevin Maddocks with a 30 plus from Alcatraz, Savay

An early double caught at long range

flavouring that I managed to get hold of. It was then that I had renewed, instant success. I was catching fish okay on the F.M.C., but I felt it was losing its effectiveness.

The carp accepted this new flavour with gay abandon and I really started to get amongst them. So much so, in one fantastic afternoon and evening, I actually managed to land thirteen doubles from the Willow Swim – quite something in freezing conditions.

Lennie too was catching many carp. He was using liquidised squid at the time which, again, was a marvellous attractor. He was always experimenting, never resting on his laurels. I believe the experiments gave him as much pleasure as actually catching the carp.

Another famous carp angler by the name of Geoff Kemp had also settled on Darenth for the winter. He, along with Kevin Maddocks, was fishing two or three days during the week and certainly, Kevin and Geoff were catching just as many, if not more than, Lennie and myself. They seemed to have the advantage of being on the water when it wasn't frozen over! Both Kevin and Geoff were on one of Geoff's own new flavours – the now very famous Dairy Cream – which has gone on in recent years to take many hundreds of fish all over the country.

Kevin was obviously still using the hair rig and still striking immediately; his catch rate was quite phenomenal. In fact, I believe that Kevin is probably one of the most 'mechanical' anglers I have ever seen; so intense about his carp fishing that he had little time for anything else on the bank; no time at all was ever wasted on idle chatting. He would be sitting over the rods all the time, waiting for that indicator to move. He really popularised the use of setting a bedchair right next to the rods and would often strike and play a fish whilst still in a sleeping bag. Even in the winter, if the night was clear, he wouldn't even use an umbrella. That winter Kevin went on to catch an incredible 84 doubles including ten twenties between November and March!

Meanwhile, Geoff didn't know anything about the hair rig, but he had a very efficient set up all of his own and was the first angler I ever saw using a fixed lead at long range. There were times, however, when I know this set up caused problems as well, for at the time we did not have the advantage of using heavy monkey climb bodies to show up dropbacks. It was the trend to use very light monkey indicators furnished out of pieces of plastic, so when a carp ran towards you on this fixed lead set up, it was very difficult to get indication at the angler's end. Geoff, being a thinking angler, did not let this deter him – he ended up using two leger weights on the line instead of the one. He would use a one ounce lead fixed on the line with a second ounce lead that was free running behind, so he had the best of both worlds. Geoff was also using quite long-shanked eyed hooks that he spent absolutely ages honing to a perfect point. Again, he was fishing quite small boilies on the eye of the hook with a short hook link, so all of us, each in our own way, had created some sort of self hooking set up. I remember looking on at some of the other anglers who were lagging behind and they just could not understand the type of takes we were getting, especially in the depths of winter. It was quite remarkable the difference these very effective set ups were making, for the rest of the anglers were still getting only twitch type takes. Very rarely did they get anything that could come close to any of the takes that we were receiving.

The enthusiasm that Lennie had for this experimentation that he was always doing really rubbed off on me. It became almost a compulsion to try something different and it was again during the winter, around Christmas time, that I started using buoyant baits; pop ups as we know them today.

Several seasons before, while fishing at Brooklands, I noticed a chap there using a floating cake, suspended on about a nine inch hook link straight off the bottom. This helped him catch one or two more fish than the others around him.

I thought that this type of set up might work very well at Darenth. I tried many ways of creating a boilie so that it would actually float. I eventually settled on rolling the paste round a square of polystyrene so

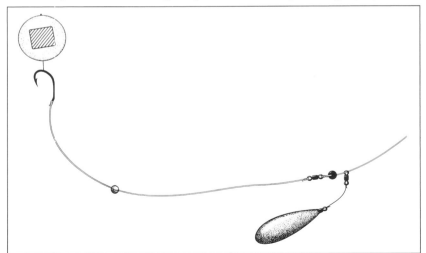

The first 'pop-up' – perhaps? A polystyrene square inserted into a boilie

that from the outside, all the baits looked exactly the same; the same diameter, the same colour and the same texture, but obviously, the one with the polystyrene would float.

In conjunction with this, I was trying all different lengths of hook link with the hair rig and eventually ended up with a very successful combination. I was fishing a pop up, suspended two inches off the bottom, counterbalanced with a couple of B.B. shots on a ten inch hook link with a 2oz lead free running on the mainline.

The hair itself consisted of a short piece of one pound breaking strain line, threaded through the centre of the boilie and tied off, and then the other end tied to the bend of the hook. The distance between the hook and the boilie was about one and a half inches. This was fished against the standard bottom bait on the other rod, with a similar length set up, and the pop up set up outfished the bottom bait by two to one. Lennie, of course, was still experimenting. He had this idea that the hair rig was more important than the bait itself and therefore he would try all manner of different boilies to prove the point; some of the concoctions he came up with quite amazing! If it could be liquidised, made into a powder, or pulped into a paste, it was made into a boilie and used on the hair. Just after Christmas, with all the left over cake and mince pies, these too ended up as boilies, along with marzipan and just about everything else from the remaining scraps of the festive dinner.

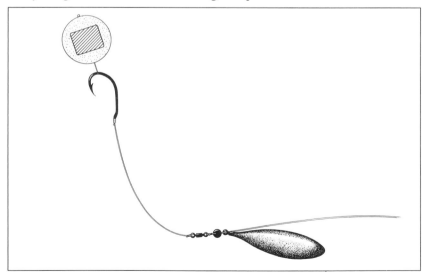

'Pop-up' fished straight up off the lead

6 -- Savay
an Opportunity Taken

Because of the friendship that I struck up with Lennie Middleton and his little group of anglers, I was fortunate enough to be invited into the syndicate that was to be formed at Savay. It was Bob Davis, one of Lennie's friends, who I also became quite friendly with whilst fishing Darenth, who was trying to organise this particular project, along with Graham Rowles who was the fishery manager at the Redlands controlled water. I had known about Savay for several years and little snippets of information always managed to drift through on the carp angling grapevine. Although very little was ever publicised about the catches, I knew in great detail the sort of stocking that had taken place there over the years.

Very few people realise that Savay started out as a trout fishery and it wasn't until the Ruislip club took over the fishing rights in the late forties that it became a coarse fishery. It was in 1950 that Savay actually received its first stocking of 300 Leney strain carp. There had been other stockings since but it was this first influx of Leney fish that really interested me, for it was known that, given the right conditions, this very exceptional strain of carp could go on and do quite tremendous things. Famous waters such as Redmire and Billing Aquadrome have produced massive carp from this particular strain. So here we have this very rich southern gravel pit that had fortunately been stocked, in my opinion, with the best type of fish available.

As you can imagine, there was very little arm twisting when it came to me being offered a place on that very first syndicate. The carp anglers who were members of the Ruislip club did such a good job of keeping their catches quiet that other than a few anglers on the select grapevine that existed in carp angling very little was known about what was actually going on there. The idea of forming a syndicate was to ascertain the potential of the carp fishing at Savay. This, with hindsight, was a bit of a joke!

Obviously, Redlands were looking to produce some extra revenue from this stretch of water and they could see that if the carp fishing potential was good, then there may be a situation there that they could capitalise on. The problem was that the way it was described to us was that this was going to be a trial and very much a one off situation. There was a very good chance then that I would only be able to fish Savay for just this one season. The timing for this could not have been worse, for up until now I had been on shift work, which had enabled me to fish for quite extensive hours during the week, but I had recently been given promotion and I was back on the eight to five stint. It certainly posed something of a problem; if I only had this one season to fish then I obviously wanted to fish for as much time as possible.

Although Savay was some sixty five acres or so in size, the syndicate was not allowed to fish all of it. In fact, I doubt if there was probably any more than about forty acres for me to choose from. It was definitely no larger than anything I had ever tackled before. That, together with the fact that Savay is split up into many small bays by islands and long peninsulas, made it seem a much smaller water than in fact it really was.

I had to think of some plan of action to get the most out of the time I had available to me. What I had decided to do was to fish every night of my rota and the weekends. I had about six weeks holiday owing to me, so all of this time was going to be devoted to fishing at Savay. I did have a few other commitments on other waters, but some of these would have to go by the wayside. They could always be fished another day.

I often wonder, when I am looking back, what the original carpers of the Ruislip club must have thought of all this, for they had had this little piece of heaven to themselves for quite some considerable time and for sure, whatever happened once the syndicate went on there, it would never, ever be the same again. I suppose all they could hope for was for us all to fail miserably, for although there were substantial stocks at Savay, it was by no stretch of the imagination, an easy water. In fact, I do know that during this time some of the original members of the Ruislip club really struggled to catch fish there.

There were two rotas and it was almost like a Who's Who of carp fishing. Bob Davis had actually picked out, to my mind, some of the best carp anglers in the country. Now if these lads weren't going to catch from Savay, I'm sure no one was.

I was very fortunate to be on the first rota, so I was going to get first crack at fishing Savay. Rota one consisted of:

Derek Cunnington	Pete Ward
Graham Marshall	Malcolm Richardson
Andy Little	John Dunn

Bob Davis	Dave Beckett
Keith Gillings	Mike Wilson
Lennie Middleton	Rod Hutchinson
Kevin Maddocks	John Webb
Graham McCulum	

Rota two was:

Paul Bray	Roger Smith
John Richards	James McCulum
Bob Harper	Sam Gates
Tony Howles	Keith Sellick
Geoff Kemp	Paul Allen
Albert Romp	Clive Dietrich
Bob Baker	Malcolm Winkworth

Certainly this was a force to be reckoned with and, in my opinion, I don't think any water, up until that time, would have had so much pressure exerted on it as these anglers were about to put on Savay.

By the time the rotas were drawn up and we'd had a couple of meetings for the rules and regulations and, of course, parted with our money, there was very little of the close season left and I felt there was much work to be done. I would just have to put myself out so every spare moment I had for the rest of the close season, was spent on the banks of Savay. The time was consumed by plumbing the depths and looking for fish and just gently trying to get to know the place. Although at first the sheer size of the water did not seem to be a daunting prospect, I found so many favourable areas that all of them could not be possibly covered.

From my close season observations, the same fish could be seen at one end of the lake one day and the opposite end the next day, so they were going to move around a lot. Although there were odd bands of residential fish, the bulk of them seemed to move on either because of weather conditions or bankside activity. This again, I thought may be something of a problem for suddenly, a water that had experienced very little pressure was about to be descended upon by a band of very proficient carp anglers. I'm sure there were many swims at Savay, prior to the syndicate, that had hardly seen an angler during the whole of the season.

I was confronted by some marvellous sights towards the start of the season. From vantage points high above the water, I observed two or three large shoals of carp, containing in excess of fifty fish. There were very few of these fish that looked under 20lb. In fact, I would have said the majority of them were over 25lb, with a lot over 30lb. This, I had never seen anywhere before. I was spellbound, just watching these huge shoals of very large carp moving up and down this beautiful water.

It was very difficult making up my mind exactly how I was going to approach the water in terms of bait. I knew that in the past successful anglers such as Mike Wilson had had some tremendous catches by fishing on particles, obviously at very close range. There were a number of swims that actually screamed out at you that they were going to be good for this type of approach. My only problem was that in the back of my mind I kept thinking that all of a sudden there was going to be a great deal more bankside activity and would the carp respond in the same way? Of course, during the quiet of the close season, the fish were very much present in the margins and on the surface of it, this looked like the obvious place to fish, but after much wrestling in my mind I actually decided to do the opposite and try to find a couple of likely areas where I could fish at reasonably long range.

What I was hoping for was to try to get the edge over the other guys, remembering that they were all proficient anglers – so I had to do something completely different. I did know, after talking to one or two of them during the course of the close season, it was going to be a full frontal approach on the particles that most of them were going to adopt, so I sorted out three different areas in various parts of the lake that I could fish fairly comfortably at long range against particular features.

My favourite was along the first part of the Canal Bank. There was a confluence of bars that all finished up on quite a large plateau just in front of an area known as Alcatraz. Now here the lake split into a Y – the right hand side of it going into the North Bay, while the left hand side went down through the channel and eventually ended up in Cottage Bay. Any carp moving up and down the lake would have to make up their minds which way they were going to go, either into the North Bay or into the channel and beyond. Therefore it seemed logical that this would be a good interception point.

As a back up, there was another area in the Cottage Bay itself. Here was a very large bed of zebra mussels, and I'm sure it was a natural feeding area as well as another stop off point on their way in and out of the Cottage Bay. At the other end of the lake, the southern end, there was a swim which came to be known as The Birches. Here the water narrowed down and there was another confluence of bars, ending up in quite a few dead ends. I was sure that with a good northerly wind blowing, the carp would end up down there. These then were really the three areas I was going to concentrate on, so regardless of weather conditions and bankside activity, I would have a choice.

The plateau out in front of the Alcatraz area looked to me to be the most favourable spot in all the lake, the problem being that there was no actual swim from which it could be fished. So, very carefully, I made myself a swim in the reeds, just enough for rods and bedchair. I could now set about a baiting up programme and for the rest of the close season, instead of walking the banks and doing any more plumbing, the time was devoted to rolling bait and actually baiting up.

The bait I was to use was going to be very similar to the one I had used at Darenth during the previous winter. The distance I would be fishing would be roughly the same so I knew that the mix and the size of the baits that I was rolling could easily cope with baiting up the Alcatraz area. I had slightly changed the original mix which was quite a good protein mix of Casein, Lactalbumin, Calcium Casinate and Gluten etc. In the new mix I had substituted some of the lighter milk protein powder with Semolina, so I ended up with the heavier Casein, Semolina and Gluten. This was bound together with eggs and could be made up to quite a solid bait which would stand being catapulted a considerable distance without flattening or breaking up. The attractor was again the Maple – this was a marvellous flavour that I had great success on during the latter part of the winter at Darenth. I was using quite a lot, up to about 20ml in a 10oz mix, and also quite a bit of sweetener; there was very little concentrated sweetener about at the time, but by diluting ordinary granulated sugar in a pan of boiling water I was able to get the concentrated solution and this I used to sweeten the mix.

It was quite funny really, because obviously there were a lot of the other syndicate members milling around during this latter part of the close season and, naturally, we discussed the sort of tactics that we were going to use. Although I kept a fair bit to myself, I did say that I was going to fish it at long range on boilies and most of them thought I was absolutely mad! Because they were all observing the fish in the margins and they had been caught there they wondered why on earth I was going to fish at long range, when they were seemingly so catchable in the margins. I was just hoping that I hadn't got it completely wrong and I was going to end up looking a right berk whilst everyone else was stacking them up under their rod tips.

There was an opportunity to go in with one or two of the other guys, but I opted to do my own thing. I did, however, keep having this inkling at the back of my mind that perhaps I had got it wrong. The rest of the lads were certainly very good anglers and all, in their own right, had done exceptionally well on many waters up and down the country and I'm sure a lot of them were far more experienced than me. Anyway, I was now committed to doing my own thing and I would have to see it through, come hell or high water. Mapping out the water was a mammoth task; I did spend a lot of time with rod and reel, legerweight and float but it was so time consuming that I needed to do the job much more quickly. To be honest, although I probably shouldn't be saying this, I ended up getting in the water myself and in fact swam over most of it, feeling for the features with my feet. Of course, this was during the close season and I was doing it quite late in the evening, so I could not be seen. It was quite interesting and is one of the best ways of getting to know a water where you can actually do it. There are so many bars in Savay that a lot of the areas are just like a ploughed field, and the side of the bars are incredibly steep. The interesting thing was that many of the bars actually joined each other, so what you would have would be two bars running parallel to each other and then ending up in a V shape as they both joined together. Now this end of these long troughs, between the two bars that were joining, had to be a really good area because there was so much food that had accumulated there.

There was one of these in front of the Reedy swim, at about fifty yards, so there was a second area I could fish as well as the distant plateau. There were plenty of areas, however, where I just couldn't get down deep enough to find out exactly what was there, so I was still unable to cover the whole area, but I found enough of interest to suit exactly what I was going to do. These much deeper areas were of very little interest to me – at the start of the season anyway.

So, with the end of the close season rapidly approaching, I had done all the mapping out that I wanted to do and had got a fair number of baits introduced into the water I'm glad to say the carp were already responding to my baiting up, which really started to give me a little bit of encouragement.

I was aware that there were more large carp at Savay than I had ever seen in my life, although of course I didn't know exact numbers. You have to remember that up until then, for the whole of my angling career, I had only caught five thirty pounders. I say only – I was very pleased with my results, but I had been used to fishing waters which, at best, had maybe one or two thirties and a handful of twenties. I was now confronted with a situation that there were many more twenties; I really didn't know how many, certainly many more than I had ever seen anywhere, and also there was a very large percentage of thirty pounders.

During my close season observations I had seen as many as maybe ten fish that could have possibly been over thirty pounds, so this was something quite exciting and incredible. I was aware of the potential and there were times that, just looking at the fish, I was shaking at the thought of putting a hook anywhere near so many large carp.

My first session on the water was on the first day of the season. As I said before, I was very lucky that I was on the first rota, so this was an opportunity I was certainly not going to let pass by. I had originally planned to start at Longfield with a friend of mine, Dave Reekie, and then move on to Darenth later on in the season but, of course, this had to go by the wayside – the call of Savay was just too great.

Lennie, for some reason or another, was not quite so optimistic as I was about Savay and he decided that he was going to start at Waveney and carry on his trials where he had left off at Darenth. Both Kevin and Lennie had done extremely well at the Waveney Valley complex a couple of seasons before and I think he really wanted to get himself in front of a lot of responsive fish, just to keep his experimentation going. You have to remember that there were very few people who knew what was going on, and I was very lucky to be part of this little band of very innovative anglers.

From what I could make out, there was probably going to be at least three quarters of the rota there on the first day of the season. It was going to be quite interesting to see how they all fared.

Mind you, I really got stitched up that first day! Bob Davis told me that there was very little point in getting there until about 4.00 p.m. on the 15th June as the gate would be closed and the lock that was on there would have a different key. So I thought rather than waste a day, I would actually do a day's work, therefore giving myself another day later in the season. I suppose it was somewhere around half past three, quarter to four when I arrived at Savay on the afternoon of the 15th and to my amazement, I found the gate open. I was even more amazed when I drove down to the car park to find it almost full!

You can imagine the sort of things that were going through my mind at that point. With so many people there, I really wondered if I would get a swim in any of the three areas I had in mind. I could see that one of the swims over on the Cottage Bank had already been taken, so there were only the other two areas which I fancied, that might be free. It was quite a long walk round to the Canal Bank, so I thought I might as well load up my gear and take it anyway. There were sure to be one or two spots down there, even if I couldn't get my little Reedy swim.

As I made my way past Alcatraz I could see that Bob Davis and Keith

Gillings were already set up. As I turned the corner into the North Bay, the Norfolk lads were making themselves comfortable, so at least this would mean there would be less people down on the Canal Bank, so I felt that I had a chance.

There was no one at all along the Canal Bank adjacent to the North Bay, and it wasn't until I reached Mike Wilson's swim that any other spots had been taken. Now Mike's was a swim to end all swims – he had been fishing here for two or three seasons and he had really made it comfortable for himself. He had nice cover in front with some beautiful iris, duck boards which were put down to stop him getting muddy feet, and the rest of the swim was turfed and cut. Mike's set up had to be one of the best prepared that I had ever seen; rods were all set out perfectly, rod mats and indicators, spare rods to the side and landing net positioned. If that wasn't bad enough, he had already got a very professional looking two and a quarter square camera set up on a tripod stand. He was obviously going to do the business! I was very much aware of the sort of success that Mike had had previously. In fact, during our one or two meetings throughout the close season, he had been quite open about his tactics and the sort of fish he had caught. He had been using particles, mainly maize, and using this as a carrier for some very special flavours he had been playing about with.

He obviously knew the topography of Savay very well, because we had quite a discussion about many of the features that abound within this lake. In fact, his own swim, which was on the east bank of the North Bay, looked perfect. There was a small island to the right, with a long bar leading off it, and a plateau some way to the left. All of this was only a few rod lengths out from the bank. These features acted as a natural funnel for fish moving in and out of the North Bay, so to my mind, he had chosen this spot very well.

I had a quick chat with Mike, but he could obviously see that I was itching to get started. He gave me the good news that there was no one in the little Reedy swim, so I could breath a sigh of relief. Just as I approached the swim the heavens opened, so it was up with the umbrella and on with the kettle. Mike came along for a chat and we sat there under the umbrella and, while sipping our tea, talked about the many different lakes that we had fished over the years. Eventually, we got around to Savay itself and just how I was going to approach it. He looked at my set up, with my 2oz leads and fast taper rods and was quite mystified about the whole thing – remember, he had been quite open about his method and I suppose he was wondering why I wasn't following suit. When I showed him the thousands of three quarter inch diameter boilies that I was about to use, he was completely horrified.

The rods were basically the same as those I was using at Darenth the season before. All I had done was that I had changed over from the original green Clooper blanks from Going Brothers, to the newer, slightly more upmarket black Conoflex Cloopers. These were still very fast taper jobs, ideal for this distance fishing that I was doing. By then I had gone on to the Cardinal 66X reels which, at the time, I honestly believed were the best available. The problem was that these came in a peculiar bronzy brown colour with a cream flier to the spool. This was, of course, during the ultra cult period and this just would not do, so these were painted matt black to match the rods. The spools of the Cardinals were overfilled with 8lb Sylcast line. This I used straight through the hook link as well, for I was positive they could not be tackle-shy fish. A 2oz lead and a size 6 Au Lion d'Or hook completed the set up. I intended to use pop ups on one rod and bottom baits on the other.

Of course, the one thing I didn't tell Mike about was the hair rig, which was still relatively unknown. I would think that, during opening week at Savay, besides Keith Gillings, Bob Davis and myself, there was no one else on it at all. I think this was something else that Mike Wilson also found a little strange, for he had revealed that Savay fish were peculiar feeders and he was strongly of the opinion that you very rarely got a run from the Savay carp at all. In fact, most of the fish that he had caught were from hitting twitches, even when the carp were preoccupied on his maize bait, so how on earth was I going to contend with hitting twitches at a ninety yard range?

Of course, I was fairly sure that I knew what the takes were going to be like! The combination of using the hair on a fairly short link with a 2oz lead and clipping up tight and I was sure that most of the takes were going to be as blistering as they were at Darenth. I had intended to use pop ups just on the one rod but as it turned out, the takes were definitely more forthcoming on this particular set up so it did not take me long to use both rods on an almost identical rig. The only difference was that I was fishing about four inches off the bottom with one, and the other varied from anything from six inches to 2 feet – just to see what sort of reaction there was. Of course, the other factor that I'm sure contributed to the success, was that for most of the time I had a great deal of bait out there. Because the pop ups stand out like a sore thumb over the top of these vast beds of bait, I'm sure that many times these are actually taken first. Probably I would have eventually got takes on the bottom baits, but I think it would have been at the stage when most of the free offerings had been cleared up, or certainly the vast majority of them.

With the pop ups, the takes were just that much quicker. Something that worried me a lot was that I had seen these very large shoals of carp swimming around and I felt, even with a thousand boilies, they could drop down on a baited area and a thousand could be gone in a matter of minutes. If that was the case, I would not be able to hold them, so I really felt that I had to put a lot of bait out there if I was going to hold these fish in one area. I suppose it was really a case of putting all my eggs in one basket and I went for it in a very big way.

Mike left the swim and I spent the next two hours catapulting bait out. What Mike must have thought of all this, I hate to think, but when he came back for our final cup of tea before the start, he did comment on just how many baits I had put in! We had another cup of tea and chatted until around 10 o'clock, when Mike returned to his swim. He wished me well and said we would have another chat in the morning.

I could hear some of the other lads casting out and setting their indicators but I thought, no, I will hang on for a little bit longer and – guess what – have a cup of tea – but you know what it's like, it eventually gets to you and really, I couldn't wait any longer. It was 11 o'clock and I whacked them out. Although my expectations were really high, I did think with all that bait I had put out I would get a good kip until morning.

I had just started to make myself comfortable, getting the bedchair and sleeping bag arranged, when crack! – out of the clip and a real flyer. As I closed the bail arm, there was certainly no need to strike as this fish was really flying. Over went the rod and even at ninety yards I had to give line immediately. After quite a scrap, the fish eventually rolled into the net. In the dim light of the torch I could see it was a magnificent looking leather and at 19lb 12oz I was over the moon. What a start – it wasn't even 12 o'clock and I had one on the bank.

There was no sacking at Savay and I for one wasn't going to take any chances. I was half hoping that Mike had heard the commotion and would come along, but I was not going to bother him at this moment, especially when the season hadn't really started. A quick photo on the floor and back she went. I thought that if anyone said anything I would just have to work out something a bit later.

I recast the rod and pulled the line back into the clip again. It started to rain again so I sat under the brolly on the bedchair for a while. I was just starting to think about getting into the bag when bang! – the other rod was away. By now it was just after midnight. This was absolutely ridiculous – this was meant to be a hard water. In an hour, two takes; another good scrap and yet another leather, this time 21lb. I remember thinking, 'sorry Mike, but I'm going to need to have a photograph of this one'. My first twenty from Savay, I couldn't let this one pass me by so I crept round and I think I frightened the life out of him! He was crouched low over his rods, twitcher hitting as you can imagine.

I told him that I had a twenty and would he please come along to do the photographing for me. He said he would be pleased to do so. He reeled in and we both crept back to the swim. He seemed to be quite amazed that I had caught a fish so quickly; I didn't have the heart to tell him that I had caught a nineteen already. I thanked him for taking the photos and we both settled down again. It seemed as if I had only just closed my eyes when, around 3.00 a.m. my right hand rod was screaming at me again. Now this fish felt completely different from the first two – nowhere near as fast, but much more determined. It chugged away to my right, down towards Alcatraz and I had to give at least fifty yards of line on that initial run. I appeared to be making no impression. I now had at least one hundred and fifty yards of line out and was really getting worried. I bent down hard and the fish started to kite in, to my right. I think it must have kited right into Mike's swim and I pumped and pumped and the fish just crashed into the margins some fifty yards down the bank to me. I leant over the water as far as I could, trying to increase the angle and eventually I did manage to get it away from the margins. It slowly circled round in front of me. By now it was pouring with rain and I was soaked to the skin. I'm glad to say it went into the net first time, but as I tried to lift the net I knew I had something quite special. I heaved it onto the bank, sorted out the scales and weigh bag and hoisted if aloft. 31lb 12oz. I was shaking like a leaf!

This was my sixth thirty. However, this was the first one I had taken at long range. Almost all my other thirties had been stalked and this, for me, was quite a mammoth fight, lasting at least forty minutes, perhaps more. Bearing in mind, I hadn't seen the fish at all; as far as I was concerned, it could have been anything, I really didn't know. Most of my other carp I'd actually seen before I'd hooked them and very often the fight would be short lived, over in a matter of minutes; but this one was on relatively light tackle at long range and was probably one of the longest fights that I had experienced. My arms were aching, but I was obviously over the moon.

The twenties that I had caught at Darenth at long range were nothing like this. Slow, dogged, determined – call it what you like. If I hadn't felt its head every now and again I would have been mistaken into thinking it had been foul hooked. It was very, very exciting and I just had to go and get Mike again. I had no other choice.

I crept along to Mike, apologising beforehand, and I remember him saying, 'You haven't got another one have you? It's not another twenty pounder is it?'

'No', I said. 'It's a thirty, Mike'.

'Oh my God!' he exclaimed.

He obviously must have been quite impressed, because he brought his own two and a quarter square camera down and I was very grateful for this, because at the time I only had a little Mickey Mouse 110 compact camera and certainly, my photographs were nowhere near as good as his. We slipped the fish back and he patted me on the back and said that he had honestly thought that I would never catch anything – and now I had caught two. I thought I'd better tell him about the nineteen pounder as well, just in case he had heard anything. I suppose there may have been a little bit of showing off as well – I think we're all a bit guilty of this from time to time.

By the morning I had caught two more – 20lb 10oz and 17½lb. Now what can I say? It was a hell of a start to the season, especially on the new water. If this was the standard of things to come, who knew what was going to happen? In fact, it just got better and better, for some of the catches were quite amazing. By the end of the first week alone, I had

A superbly scaled whacker

fourteen fish.

It was quite amazing. I'd had a personal best of 34lb 4oz, which beat my old previous best of 33lb by a considerable margin. I'd also had a personal best common of 24lb. In fact, this was my first ever 20lb common and I shall never forget that fish.

A local guy, John Richards, who was on the other rota, had wandered round to see me. Obviously, the other lads had told him about my catches and seeing there was very little else coming out he was keen to find out just what he had got to do to catch fish. I'd never met John before, but by the end of the season at Savay he turned out to be a very good friend.

It was change-over day and John asked if he could slot in next to me. I said, of course, no problem at all. There were obviously a lot of fish out there and they were taking a lot of baits. John had done a fair bit of long range fishing, but was certainly not on the hair.

We stood behind the swim, chatting to each other, when a good fish crashed out over my baits. It looked very much like it was a common and he agreed. There were one or two good fish in there that were commons, one of them known to be just under thirty. At that time I had not taken a common anywhere near that size.

As we stood there chatting I had another take – the indicator just zipped off, it was a blur. I had another hell of a struggle, this one being quite fast, dashing around all over the place. John helped me with the netting and, because of the surroundings in the swim, I was back up the bank while he was down at the water's edge, and I couldn't actually see the fish. Just as it went in the net, he said 'You've got a twenty pound common'.

Well, that really was the icing on the cake and definitely a week I shall never forget.

The other lads unfortunately, really struggled. Mike Wilson did have a 28lb leather during the course of the opening week, but I honestly believe that I had so much bait out in front of me that I was holding the fish back and they were not going into Mike's swim. I think only one or two fish slipped through and this was probably one of the fish that he had caught.

The rest of the lake produced virtually nothing. Rod managed to get the carp going on the top before the off, but they had dwindled away and disappeared. He did manage to get a double, a sixteen pounder I think, on Maples, but during that first week the rest of the anglers certainly struggled. They obviously realised the potential and when some of them did get their act together, some of the catches were quite staggering. I

First from Savay

An incredible fish caught on maple flavour

Tired, wet, but very happy

20 plus common taken early morning at Burton

learnt a lot during that first week.

I thought I could bait up quite well after the fishing at Darenth, but this was completely different. Although the range was roughly the same, Darenth being a smaller water and that much more sheltered, the baits were fairly unaffected by winds, but in my little reedy swim the water out in front was quite open and the strong south westerlies would have the baits flying everywhere. It showed just how inadequate I was at putting bait out at long range. This was prior to the wrist-rocket days, so really all we had was the basic, standard type catapults with square elastics and a home made pouch. Latex was just not available at the time. The amount of catapult elastic I went through was just ridiculous. There were times when I had to beg, steal or borrow from the other members just to keep the bait going in. In fact, it was Rod who first introduced me to the Latex elastic. He had been given some to try on what was called a 'Whopper Dropper' catapult. I think this was meant for putting out large balls of groundbait and I remember him saying 'You won't bust this one!' – but after a couple of thousand baits this too, broke, so he was none too pleased with me, as you can imagine.

I had to find something different that was going to last a little bit longer and it was in one of the gun shops that I found a hunting catapult, called a 'Marksman', which was an American made job. It was very strong and much more accurate, but I was still using four or five lengths of Latex per day. You hear people glibly saying that they have put a thousand baits out: well, I can assure you it takes a very long time to put that many baits out with a catapult, as I was doing on a daily basis.

After that first week was over I felt sad that I had to go away. I had arranged to meet Lennie on the Monday, and also my friend, Dave Reekie, down at Darenth. I packed up and I met Bob Davis in the car park. He obviously realised that I was keen to carry on and the response on the other rota had not been that great so he said that if I could find someone to swap rotas then I could carry on fishing, he didn't mind. This worked out very well and I took advantage of it.

One of John Richard's friends, Bob Harper, was on the other rota and for some reason or other, didn't actually end up fishing there at all. I managed to persuade him to let me have his ticket and obviously if he did want to fish there, I would give it back at any time. This he kindly agreed to do, so I was able to fish all the time from there on. It's a much harder water than most people realise. When it's on song it is like a lot of waters, it can look very easy, but it wasn't easy all the time. You've only got to look at some of the other guy's catches for proof of that. There were some very proficient anglers there who really struggled to catch fish and because the carp at Savay generally proved to be shoal fish, one, maybe two people, could get on fish but there was no way that twenty five were going to.

In the end there was probably less than half the rota who fished seriously, so at least this did allow the guys who wanted to fish full time to do so, as they were able to swap with those who didn't fish.

I naturally wanted to stay on at Savay, especially as it was going so well, but I had arranged to go to Darenth, so off I went. Once the Savay season was in full swing, what usually happened was that once all my holidays were exhausted, I would leave for work around 7.00 a.m. – it was between forty and fifty miles drive from Savay to work, depending on which way I went. Once I arrived at work I would have a shower, eat breakfast and make a few baits. Lunchtime too was bait making time too, but at least I was able to have a good meal virtually every day. I would arrive back at Savay between 6 and 6.30 p.m., depending on the traffic. I was very fortunate that there were many times when I was able to leave my tackle at the back of the swim. I obviously wouldn't occupy it, but when Lennie or Rod were about they would just keep an eye on it for me. If I was on fish, I would naturally return to the place I had left in the morning, but if not, I would spend much of the evening looking for visual sightings. Also, the other lads who were present would fill me in with all the info by the time I got back because as the season wore on, both Rod and Lennie were spending a great deal of time there. It was a friendly atmosphere and if you had a particular swim going no one would jump in it the moment you vacated it. They would leave it alone – which something you just don't get these days. I must admit, I did feel quite guilty at times, when I was really on the fish and they would leave it vacant all day until I got back in the evening. There is something to be said for this type of friendship.

A lot of the time would be spent baiting up, just to ensure that there was a constant food supply for the carp to drop in on any time. I could never make enough bait up at work to see me through the day, so there was still bait making to be done on the bank, virtually every day.

Because I was working every weekday I would try to get my head down by 11 o'clock at night at the latest, as I had to be up early to be at work.

There were many nights when the carp did not respond at all. In fact, what would generally happen was that there would be long periods of inactivity followed by short, hectic spells of feeding. Several fish would come in the same night. If these feeding times coincided with weekdays, there were moments, believe it or not, when I dreaded them! It was often the case that they would feed all night: I would get no sleep at all and often be late for work – inevitably getting a telling off in the process. At times it was hard work and I just felt like going home, going to bed and getting away from it all. However, this was going to be a one off and I had to put myself out if I was going to do well, for there was a chance I would never fish Savay again. I was determined to make the best of it. As the season progressed, I was beginning to have pressures exerted on me that I didn't particularly want. Because I was doing so well, and through the friendship that I had with the others on the bank, they were all spurring me on to catch even more fish. Somehow or other I seemed to have got wound up in this numbers syndrome. I'm not quite sure how it happened and I was surprised that I was actually getting myself involved in it. Kevin Maddocks had had a great season the year before and was the first person I knew of to catch twenty twenties in a season. This appeared to be some sort of target that he set; quite silly in hindsight, because it's all relative; hours, water, ability etc., but I was egged on to catch more fish. I had gone through the twenty twenties barrier fairly early in the season. It was then twenty five twenties, thirty twenties and, quite honestly, it was just getting ridiculous. It was pressure that I felt I didn't really need; I just wanted to enjoy myself and not thrash the water to death. It turned out to be a ridiculous season and I'm the sort of person who tries hard anyway, regardless of whether the fish are feeding or not. Anyway, back to the beginning of the season. After the first week I went to Darenth and told Lennie of my success: I was all fired up with the enthusiasm there and now Lennie was all raring to go. The next trip, when we were there together, I was in my little Reedy Swim and Lennie went out onto the area at the end of Alcatraz so that we could fish on virtually the same hotspot but from different positions in the lake. It was a much longer cast from the end of Alcatraz than it was from the Reedy Swim, and although he did catch from there, the Reedy Swim was a much better vantage point and Lennie never quite had as many fish.

It was really funny, because after that session the carp avoided that area for quite some time. I remember Lennie staying put there for something like a week, even though I do believe the fish had moved off. I went round to the Cottage Bay where there were some more carp showing. John also joined me around this area. This is a part of the lake that you can't actually fish these days, which is a shame because it's a lovely little area. We fished round outside the cottage itself; there were a lot of fish moving into the Cottage Bay, I think they had slipped through the channel and had congregated in large numbers just off the islands at the entrance to Cottage Bay.

By now I had got quite friendly with John and I asked him if he fancied coming in on the bait with me. This was for two reasons; one, I obviously wanted John to catch fish and secondly, at least someone else could help with making this ruddy bait! I was in something of a dilemma however. Although I was quite happy to tell him about the bait I was using, I was still sworn to secrecy on the hair and I stuck to it, even though I felt bad about it at times. I'm sure John realised something strange was going on but he accepted it and did not ask too many questions.

The first session round in Cottage Bay we put a stack of baits out – round about 7,000 between us. I think it was the next day when the fish actually moved onto the bait. John was at the head of the swim and he was first in, using fairly standard rigs. I remember thinking at the time, 'I wonder what is going to happen when they finish up at my end of the swim with the hair rig and all'. This was John's first Savay fish he was hooked into and, as usual, it was a really good scrap and it turned out to be a thirty pound plus. I remember kidding him that it was only a double and he should stop messing about and get it in. Rod had come round and was looking over our shoulder and even when the fish was four feet down in the water he said, 'Blimey, it's another thirty!'

Lennie Middleton and Andy with a magnificent quartet

Then it really started to happen. The next day I had a brace of thirties in consecutive casts; it just went on and we held the fish there for quite some time.

A brace of thirty pounders had to be special at any time, it really was quite something – this is probably going to sound awful – but it was all starting to get a bit too easy and I was almost becoming blasé about it. I'd never had it so good, never had so many big fish in front of me and never put so many on the bank. I remember catching fish in the twenty five pounds bracket and thinking, 'that's a nice fish, but I wonder if the next one will be an upper twenty or thirty'. This area round the Cottage Bay seemed to be almost better than out in front of the Reedy Swim and I recall we really built up the swim. Late one particular night I had five fish over twenty pounds, most of them being upper twenties, in very short succession.

At first you could almost predict where the carp were going to be, according to the weather. You could hold them with baits for quite a while, but eventually a big wind pushing down would move them. In fact, this weather syndrome started up quite a bit of a lark. There would be one or two of us who would go to the phone box every day and ring up the Met. Office and try to predict exactly what the weather was going to be; in some respects it was a bit like the Secret Society. A little bit of friendly competition was now coming into play; there was a lot of secret phoning up the Met. Office and a lot of moving around in the middle of the night, trying to get to a certain area before the carp arrived.

Very often weather conditions would change during the course of the day and if a lot of bait had been eaten during the night and I had to go to work in the morning, I could get back and all the carp had moved from one end of the lake to another. There were odd occasions when the weather conditions were just right, when the major three shoals that seemed to be resident in Savay all got together in one area or another. This was quite a phenomenal sight I can tell you. It's very difficult to be precise about numbers, but I would have thought at least seventy very good carp could be present at any one time. There were two main strains of carp in Savay. There was the original Leney stocking and these were very long, streamlined fish and were very hard fighting. The best of these that season was a 34lb 4oz fish, that I managed to catch twice. In fact, it was one that Lennie caught a bit later in the season, although he didn't actually count it – but that's another story...

Then there was the Italian strain of fish – these were much shorter and fatter and I wasn't that keen on them at all. The best of these were around 28lb and included a very famous fish that ended up being called

'Popeye'. I don't think any of the Italians went over thirty pounds during that first season and I'm fairly sure 'Popeye' was the biggest of them all.

There were a few commons in the twenty pound bracket as well, the largest of which was the one called 'Sally'. This was a fish that you could recognise instantly as there was a half moon shaped lump missing from the tail. This was a fish that Mike Wilson had caught at just under 30lb the previous season, but during the course of our year it was down slightly in weight and Paul Bray caught it at about 27lb. When you think that fish today (1990) is nearly 40lb., it is quite remarkable. Sadly, I never caught Sally myself; I think it was the only one of the big fish that I didn't catch. I captured two other 20lb commons there; a 24lb and a 26lb but it would have been really great if I had caught Sally as well. However, it was not to be and I suppose, at the end of the day, I caught so many fish did it really matter?

As the season progressed, inevitably the hair rig started to get out. In actual fact, I was caught using it by Sam Gates. He saw me striking into a fish and came round to help. This was during one of my bumper sessions when everything started to click together and I was absolutely stacking them up. I'd only just caught another carp a few minutes beforehand; I had baited up my rig and was about to cast out when I had a take on the other rod, so there it was, lying against the bedchair for the world to see and of course, as Sam came round the corner there it was, staring him in the eyes. The thoughts of netting my fish went completely out of the window – all he was interested in was looking at this peculiar set up!

Having been caught red handed with it, there was no way I was going to lie, so I came clean. I told him it was not mine, but Lennie and Kevin's idea and said that he really must keep it to himself. Of course, like all good things, inevitably they do get out and I thought we had done quite well in keeping it quiet for so long!

I was still fishing every evening – that continued right through until November. I did have the odd couple of days off the water, but not that many. It was certainly a very expensive season; I could not have done it if I had been unemployed. The cost of petrol, bait, food and everything else was taking its toll. I even changed the bait to a much cheaper and simpler mix of just semolina and gluten to try to save a bit of money. I still carried on with the Maple flavour and the sweetener but nothing else – quite amazing really.

I was on size 8 Au Lion d'Or hooks, which were quite small compared to the size of the baits, which were roughly three quarters of an inch in diameter.

Although I was paying my rent regularly at the flat, I think my land-lord wondered where on earth I had got to: I would only rarely go home and only then to get a change of clothing or to pay a few bills. I've got absolutely hundreds of memories of Savay, some funny, some sad and some just ridiculous. There is one situation I shall never forget. Lennie and I had doubled up in the Bonfire Swim at the start of what was to be a fantastic season. We were on fish immediately and the first night I think I had four takes within a very short space of time – three of which I lan-ded, the other unfortunately came off. I believe that there was at least one thirty, if not two and an upper twenty nine amongst these fish. Len-nie too, managed to put an upper twenty on the bank, so this was a really great start to the session. Up until this point, Lennie had never caught a thirty pound plus carp; plenty of twenty nines but no thirties, so obviously Savay was a real opportunity for him. Lennie, never being one to sit on his laurels, started experimenting once again, even though we were in the middle of catching fish. In all fairness, I don't think Lennie ever stopped experimenting and it was on a new rig that he got his next take.

This was on his right hand rod which was fished to the far right of the Bonfire Swim. Now this was obviously a very good fish that he had just hooked into. It kited way round to the left over Lennie's other rod, plus mine, and it was some 150 yards down the lake when it crashed into the margins. No matter how hard Lennie pulled into the fish, he was just not making any impression on it. The hooked carp just kept powering away from him; it was now right down by the Gate Swim, still in the margins, but Lennie's line was through loads of sunken branches so he had very little chance of getting the fish back to him. After a bit of quick thinking and I grabbed my spare rod and cast out between the gaps in the branches to hook his line up. I would retrieve it onto the bank where we would break it and retie. I don't know how many times this was repeated, but I do know that it was getting on for an hour later when we eventually landed the fish.

We could see immediately just what the problem was – it was foul hooked in the pectoral fin! I recognised the fish as one I had caught earlier at 34lb 4oz. I just couldn't believe it; Lennie's first thirty and the ruddy thing was foul hooked. There was a scratch and a mark in the carp's mouth, but Lennie was not happy about it and refused to count it. That just goes to show the calibre of angler that he is: I wonder how many people would have counted that fish, given the circumstances. Anyway, one thing was for sure, I was going to have a photograph of him and this fabulous fish, no matter what he said. I was very impressed by

Lennie as an angler. We were very lucky really, a nicer bunch of guys would be hard to find, but, as with any group, one or two stand out above the rest for various reasons.

As well as Lennie, there were people like Rod Hutchinson. What can you say about Rod? Rod is just Rod, quite a character and a very likeable chap and probably the most instinctive angler I have ever known. Also Kevin Maddocks whose sheer technical ability and the methodical way he approaches his fishing has to be commended. I have always thought that if you could get Lennie's forward thinking and rig craft, Rod's originality and watercraft, and Kevin Maddocks' accuracy and drive, there would be an angler in the country that no one else could possibly touch. Cor, wouldn't it be horrible?!

Good catches kept coming periodically right up until the beginning of November, then I think the sheer pressure that we were exerting upon the carp completely pushed them out of the area that we could fish. As the autumn progressed, the carp seemed to get further and further down the canal bank towards the sluices and by the beginning of November the fish that were being caught were either coming from the Birches or the Gate Swim. These were just about the last two fishable swims along the canal bank.

Eventually they moved down to the sluices and round the other side of the Ruislip island. Now this was awfully frustrating, as we could see the carp through the trees, on the far side of the island but could not put a bait to them. The catches completely dropped off and in actual fact, the last carp that I was to catch from Savay was on November 10th.

Although I went back several times throughout the winter, I neither caught, or could find, any more carp. So really that was the end of a truly phenomenal season at Savay and from June 16th until November 10th, I put forty three twenties on the bank, thirteen of these being over thirty pounds. I had never had a season like it and, to be honest, I really can't see me repeating this on any other U.K. water in the future.

It really was a case of everything coming together at the right time –the access onto one of the most prolific big fish waters in the country, virtually being the first in with the hair rig and using boilies at long range. The ironic thing is that we truly believed that this was going to be a one off and, I for one, fished my socks off. Then at the end of the season, we heard that the syndicate was to carry on and I was duly offered the chance to renew my place.

I thought about this long and hard and, in the end, decided against it. There was no way I was going to repeat the success and just how many more carp did I want to catch from Savay? I suppose there was always

Sally to go back for, but then again, I never seemed to have a lot of luck with the commons and may have fished the water for the rest of my life without bumping in to her. So in the end I declined, at least knowing that someone else would have the opportunity of fishing this marvellous water. With hindsight, I now believe that this was the right decision, for things at Savay were, inevitably, never to be the same again. I have wonderful memories of that year, with the fish I caught, the friends I made, and becoming almost a part of the bankside. I don't think I could ever have repeated such a magical time. I started to take things a bit easier after November, but still spent the weekends at Darenth, adding a few more twenties during the course of the winter and the back end. I finally ended up with a phenomenal tally of fish with two hundred and six over ten pounds, fifty of them being over twenty, including thirteen over the magical thirty. It was certainly an exhausting season, fishing a ridiculous number of hours, but I enjoyed every minute of it. I don't think I will ever put that much effort into my carp angling again. I have a much better perspective on life these days but I don't think I would have missed the experience for the world.

It just got better...

7 — Return to Longfield

I had made the decision not to return to Savay, which at least allowed me to fish other venues which I'd been planning to have a crack at before being offered a place on that first Savay syndicate. One thing was certain, there was no way I was going to repeat the catches I had at Savay. For one, I was not going to put the time in, I felt that I needed some breathing space. Unwanted pressures had been put upon me and I just didn't want to get tied up within this one-upmanship numbers syndrome. I did not like the idea of being classed within the hierarchy of the carp fraternity just by how many fish I had caught. It's a nonsense.

The other reason I wouldn't be repeating the catches was that I was not going to be fishing on such a unique water as Savay with its vast numbers of twenties and thirties. The water I had chosen to fish was Longfield. I had fished it back in the days prior to the Yeoveney fish being transferred there. At that time Longfield was a very quiet water, hard fishing, with only a handful of carp caught every year. But with the influx of the Yeoveney fish, things looked very promising with the possibility of putting one or two real lumps on the bank. Those Yeoveney fish were quite something.

There was one real cracker that I certainly had my eye on and that was the smaller of that magnificent brace of upper thirties that Pete Springate had caught. Also, my good friend Dave Reekie had spent a bit of time there himself. We had originally planned to fish it together during that 80/81 season. Events ruled that out but Dave had carried on regardless and had had a fabulous season, taking some magnificent fish. He had caught about nine fish in all, including the big leather at 35lb 12oz. This was caught on the same bait I was using at Savay, the good old Maple flavour once again. Dave was the first person to use the hair rig at Longfield – with devastating effect. It was during the close season before I fished Longfield again that I joined the B.C.S.G. This was rather ironic as I had applied several years before but was unsuccessful, but this time I was actually invited to join – just after that great season at Savay. Coincidence? I think not. However, I did want to join the group and I was not going to miss this opportunity. Even more ironic, as it turned out, it was Chris Ball who was to vet me!

Chris was, at that time, the Regional Organiser for the Surrey and Middlesex branch of the B.C.S.G. I had known him prior to this meeting, mainly through socials and branch get togethers of the Carp Anglers' Association and, of course, as always, he was keen to chat about carping exploits. If my memory serves me well, I think a meeting was arranged at 'The Toby Jug' on the A3. I arrived there clutching bundles of photo albums, wondering what to expect. Chris followed me in a few minutes later and we spent probably the next four hours chatting about carp and carp waters that we had fished. At the end of the evening, as we said our goodbyes in the car park, I think we had both forgotten what the meeting was about. I, for one, really had no idea whether I had become a B.C.S.G. member or not, such was the chatting about carping. In fact, it was a few evenings later when he rang me and said 'Oh, by the way, you did want to be a member of the group, didn't you?'

Chris really has got an insatiable appetite for carp angling and it almost seems that the older he gets the more enthusiastic he becomes. He is one of the true characters of the carping world. It was really from that meeting that we struck up a good friendship and I'm glad to say that we have fished consistently together since that time, and he has become one of my very best friends.

I had met Jan Wenczka quite a few years before. Our first meeting was when he turned up at a C.A.A. do that I was running. I believe that was over at Woking or somewhere like that. He had popped along to see Peter Mohan regarding his B.C.S.G. membership. He was also poking around down at Savay and I was trying to do my best not to let on about the catches – but Jan's no fool, I'm sure he knew exactly what was going on. However, it was through my friendship with Chris that Jan and myself became pals, as Jan and Chris had been fishing together for quite a while.

When I went back to Longfield, I was only going to do short sessions. I'd had quite enough of spending every night on the bank at Savay and I was now getting used to the comfort of my own bed.

At the beginning of the season I had planned to do some early morning sessions before work, mainly because I thought it would be a lot quieter during the week than at weekends. This would obviously allow me to move around the lake more freely, giving me a better chance to get on to the fish.

From Dave's earlier observations, during the season before, most of these chances early in the season came before about 9 o'clock in the morning, so this was a good opportunity to capitalise on what was hopefully a good feeding period – always assuming that not too much had changed. The plan was, that as the season drew on I would then probably change to weekends only, or maybe one or two evenings a week if conditions looked favourable.

As for tackle and tactics, I could see very little point in changing the bait as Dave had caught quite a lot of fish in relatively few hours and had by no means completely turned over the place on the bait. Of course, there was a good chance that they would instantly recognise it from the season before.

Longfield, at the time, was extremely weedy so this called for stout tackle. The 12ft 2¼ Tri Casts would be fine, matched with 12 or 15lb Sylcast. For most of the time I used a braided Terylene hook link in conjunction with a pop up suspended between two and four inches off the bottom. The hooks themselves were size 4 Au Lion d'Ors. The hair itself was quite short, only about half an inch between the hook and the periphery of the bait, and consisted of one pound breaking strain monofilament.

The bait was the magic Maple flavour yet again, heavily sweetened with Sucron. The base mix was a simple carbohydrate, consisting of Semolina, Rice Flour and Gluten as a binder. This was mixed up with eggs and the flavour rate was about 25ml of the Maple to one pound of dry mix.

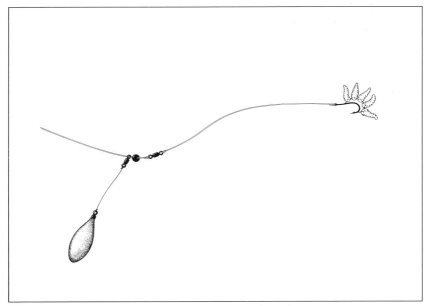

River Thames rig with maggots mounted on 5 amp fuse wire

As the season progressed, I did change the mix slightly. I wanted the bait to start breaking down more quickly, and went on to a semi Bird Food Mix, adding P.T.X. and Nectar Blend to the Semolina and Rice Powder and cutting right down on the Gluten. Also, substituting some of the eggs with water, for I had a feeling that at times there were far too many free offerings lying about uneaten. This revised mix broke down very quickly indeed, which suited me, as I was only doing short sessions anyway.

I started the season off at Longfield – and that was one hell of a mistake. Talk about a circus, it nearly put me off fishing there altogether. I decided I would get down there very late in the evening. I wanted to see the season in, but just couldn't be bothered doing a session and bivvying up, so I didn't arrive until about half past ten on June 15th. I was quite staggered to find there were only about three swims vacant. This I had not really anticipated for, asking around, as you do, in the close season, it appeared that there was only going to be the normal handful of regulars – but this was not the case at the off.

What had actually happened was that someone had arranged for a Press Day. I can't remember which paper it was now, but I think Ritchie had something to do with organising it. I don't think there was actually anything being caught, but I seem to remember a lot of photographs being taken of Ritchie's immaculate set up. 'All polished stainless and carpets'.

This was enough to make me leave it alone for the first couple of weeks until things had quietened down. When I returned, it was a very different place – I'm glad to say. At most, there would only be two or three people. Vic Gillings and Tony were doing a couple of nights a week and Ritchie was on his normal three to four day sessions, so, to be honest, this was very quiet. The weekends would naturally see more pressure so I curtailed my efforts to between Monday and Thursday morning only for the first couple of months.

There were a couple of going areas where the fish consistently showed – one in front of the Noddy swim and another in front of the Log Cabin. Both these areas I managed to take fish from.

The Pier Swim was an area where there always seemed to be someone fishing. The carp seemed to know this and although the odd fish was taken, I avoided it unless it really screamed out.

The nice thing at Longfield was that the carp could be easily observed from high vantage points in many of the climbing trees. You could look down into the clear water and watch the carp swimming in and out of the weed beds. There was the odd chance of stalking the fish and, to be honest, in some respects this could give you your best chance of hooking and landing a fish. I lost quite a few carp by casting into gaps in the weed between forty and sixty yards out. You had no control over the fish at that range and they would get so bogged down. Eventually the hook would pull, so these were really a waste of chances.

I managed to put seven fish on the bank, two of which were thirties; four of them were caught by stalking tactics, the others from the Noddy Swim or the Log Cabin. This was probably less than fifty per cent of the carp I actually hooked, so it was not a very good conversion ratio I'm afraid.

Although most of them only seemed to acquire names in later years, looking at some of the photographs they are very recognisable. There is the Koi, Heart Shaped Tail and The Lady. All of these are now known fish.

By the end of September things really started to slow up and the weekends were fairly busy, so I could not swing the opportunities in my favour. I decided that enough was enough and pulled off. After all, I'd had a fabulous time and caught far more than I really expected to, especially considering I had done very little in the way of hours. Well, certainly not fishing that is – I did spend a lot of time looking. In fact,

The result of tree-top observation, a well known Longfield biggie

there were many occasions when I went to Longfield with the idea of fishing, but after spending several hours looking, decided that it did not look favourable and went back home again.

I looked in at Longfield on a few occasions in the winter but I just didn't fancy it. I carried on fishing the Thames until the flood water pushed the carp out of the areas where I was concentrating and from then on I stuck to the Wimbledon Park lake where I just had a lot of fun with the smaller fish.

I ended the season regaining some of the sanity that I had lost at Savay and felt, at last, that the induced pressure that I had put on myself had been lifted and I was able to just enjoy what I liked best of all; just catching carp.

Thirty plus of Fox Pool carp

8 — Sanity Regained

My time was then divided between fishing the Thames and the local Wimbledon Park.

Wimbledon Park was a great saviour to me, there were just no big fish there at all. Literally hundreds of singles, a few doubles and apparently one or two twenties, although I must admit I never bumped into any. Wimbledon Park was a bit of exclusive fishing; it was fairly difficult to obtain tickets and I was fishing it as a guest of one of the members.

There was little or no pressure from carp anglers and it was a wonderful piece of fun fishing. You could have some quite amazing catches; it was nothing to catch fifteen to twenty fish in an afternoon's sport! Most of the carp ran between seven and ten pounds, with the occasional fish in the twelve to fourteen pounds bracket. On light tackle, very entertaining.

The swims there were quite something as well, for they mainly consisted of little platforms built out into the water amongst the reed beds – and this was in the days before the Rod Pods. Would they have been a blessing there! I ended up using long landing net poles as front and rear bank sticks so that the rods could be positioned just in front of these little pontoons in the water.

I chuckle to myself when I think of some of the horrendous bankside ironmongery that I used to make up to fish off the stages; great lumps of angle iron were bent in all manner of shapes to try to get some stable fixing to the woodwork. Of course, the biggest problem of fixing anything to the stages themselves was that every time you moved, or someone came to visit you, the whole lot would bounce up and down setting buzzers and indicators off, so this was not a very convenient set up. The long rod rests were fine on the stages where there was fairly shallow water, but there was one or two, especially the large main one, that went some ten or fifteen yards out into the lake, where there was over 4ft of water as well as 3ft of silt to contend with, so we had to put up with the angle iron Heath Robinson set up on that particular stage. This long stage was quite good fun at times as you would actually be fishing back towards the bank and the carp would avidly feed beneath the staging itself. Now, the staging was held up by scaffold poles every five or six feet or so and you can imagine hooking a carp in this situation; they would certainly run you a merry dance around the underwater metal work.

If you felt very daring, you could actually crawl along the staging on your stomach, with the hook bait in hand whilst your rod was left further back with the bail arm open, and gently lower a lump of floating crust literally right into the mouth of a carp, only inches from your nose. You would have to strike while the line was still in your hand, then rush back to the rod as all hell broke loose. It was undoubtedly exciting fishing!

During the summer months, most of the carp would fall to particle fishing in the more open water swims, and floaters and bread crusts fished in among the lily pads and around the landing stages themselves. Come the winter we would swop over and use boilies and the one nice thing about the Wimbledon carp was that it seemed they would feed in just about any conditions. No matter how hot or cold the weather, providing you could get a bait in the water, you were virtually guaranteed action – one of the very few places where I can honestly say I never blanked.

Session angling on this water seemed a million miles away and almost a thing of the past, as most of the fishing at Wimbledon consisted

A Wimbledon common carp

of short morning and afternoon sessions, rarely fishing into the night until winter came. As the cold weather descended upon us, the carp, for whatever reason best known to themselves, decided that they were far happier picking up baits during the hours of darkness but, luckily for me, mostly before midnight. So throughout the winter I altered my sessions so that I would fish from about five in the afternoon until ten in the evening. With baits going in regularly on an almost every other day basis, action continued on a consistent basis.

The bait for the winter, which was a lightly skinned boilie, was heavily flavoured with maple and sweetener and as the winter drew on, there was a feeling in my mind that a change of flavour may bring an extra few takes. I had, by now, noticed that the action was dropping off slightly, although I was probably still averaging four or five fish an evening. I swopped over to Blueberry flavour, again at quite a high level of 10ml per 10oz mix with 2½ml for sweetener. With little or no baiting up, this brought the extra action that I had anticipated and gave me that additional two or three takes an evening that I felt I had been missing.

It's strange, when you get to know a water very well and the moods of its inhabitants, you instinctively know when you are not getting it one hundred per cent right and the edge is not as keen as it should be and very often, just by fine tuning the end tackle, altering the baits slightly or maybe even creating a new feeding area, things can be very rapidly swung back in your favour.

Obviously, by now the hair rig had been around for a couple of seasons, but there was very little pressure on the carp, save for one or two anglers. The takes were blinding and virtually every one was converted to a fish on the bank. The poor old carp really didn't know what was happening to them. Up until now they had probably only been caught on fairly standard baits like sweetcorn, bread and maggots, on crudely set up match type tackle, either under a float or on a feeder, so to be suddenly confronted with particles, boilies and the hair rig, it took them a long time to suss out what was going on. For my part, fishing at Wimbledon Park and the Thames was a bit of escapism as I was going through a period in my life where I was getting disillusioned with the modern carp scene; the numbers game, the oneupmanship and the general conduct of anglers on the bank. I just could not face the circuit type waters, nor did I have the frame of mind for the pursuit of monster carp. I just wanted to be out there enjoying myself alone – me against the carp with little, or no, outside influence.

I imagine this would be a water which was never heard of, or known to, the diehard anglers so you can imagine my surprise when I occasionally bumped into people like Pete Springate and Ken Hodder during some of my winter evenings. Actually, it was quite nice to see anglers of this very high calibre sitting on easy waters for a bit of respite from the hard, big fish venues that they would normally be fishing.

The Thames is never easy. It's a contrary water, location being the prime problem, but there are one or two areas where there appear to be residential fish, and it was these that I fished that particular season. I managed to catch a dozen or so doubles, including one or two twenties. These were from spots like the Desborough Cut where there are a couple of twenties that come out on a regular basis. I had the smaller one at 24lb but its big brother, the 29lb completely eluded me. I photographed it three times for other people, all match anglers! It fell to maggots or casters every time.

An upper double from Hogsmeal

Another area was at Staines, where the Hogsmeal enters the Thames. This is ever such a snaggy area, all manner of rubbish seems to have accumulated here so it called for 15lb line straight through. Real hit and hold tactics. I managed a few doubles up to 17lb from this spot.

Kingston Town was also kind to me. Behind the shops, where the stream enters the river, is another hot spot which is always good for a couple of doubles, so rather than doing any pioneering work I just dropped into little areas where I had either caught fish in the past or knew of carp to be caught there.

Maggots and casters are definitely the best baits on the Thames but unfortunately not very selective, even when used in bunches on size 10 or 8 hooks. Luncheon meat, although it did catch one or two carp, just didn't produce anything near the results I expected it to. It caught lots of chub and the odd barbel, but not many carp. Sweetcorn I found to be much better, so generally I would be fishing on the corn or with the maggots and casters. I've caught very few Thames carp on boilies.

The hook baits would generally be fished over quite large beds of particles like Hemp, Tares or Mini Maples, so things were kept fairly simple.

Friends of mine, the late David Carl Forbes and Nigel Widdowson,

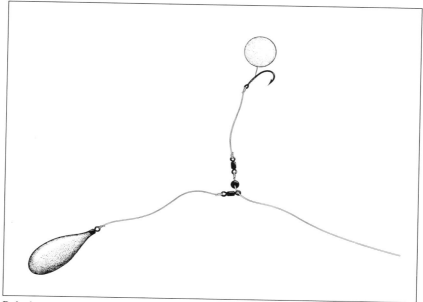

Baked pop-up – on lead forward anti-tangle rig I used at Longfield

also had varying degrees of success with Thames carp, most of which were caught whilst in pursuit of barbel. The would tell me stories of other large fish that were lost on inadequate tackle as well as big fish that would be heard crashing out during the hours of darkness. All this information compiles in the little grey cells and, occasionally, everything clicks into place on the Thames, but it does tend to be a lot of hard work. Eventually, when a fish does grace your net, there is a real sense of achievement, regardless of the size of fish. I am totally convinced that there are real monsters in the Thames, waiting to be caught, and one day a fish will definitely be landed which will open people's eyes to the true potential of the river.

For me, I was quite happy doing it on my own to gain that piece of sanity I was seeking.

9 — Peace of Mind

Longfield was starting to see a bit of pressure by this time so I joined a small syndicate called Stuart's Pond. This was run by a friend of mine, Andy Tucker, who had taken it over from a very famous barbel angler, Barry Brock, who unfortunately had died around that time.

This was a little piece of heaven really. I had wanted to get away from the rat race of the circuit waters, after the fantastic years at Savay and Longfield. Carp fishing was now becoming a very prestigious sport. There were a lot of carp anglers joining the carp fishing ranks and the waters now were really getting to see a lot of pressure.

Carp fishing had come on in leaps and bounds, certainly in the last decade and by the early 80's there were certain waters where groups of anglers were on them doing really extensive hours. It wasn't so many years ago that if an angler fished for four or five thousand hours in a season, it was seen to be almost excessive, but times were changing and there were a lot of hours being put in. I wanted to get away from it all, so I joined this little syndicate water, which was smashing.

There were only a few members fishing there and it was very small, probably no more than three acres. They were a nice, friendly bunch of lads. There was no long term fishing at all, most of it was carried out during the daytime and it was a nice stalking water with a reasonable head of fish and no monsters in it. There were a few twenties, quite a few doubles and loads of singles.

It had actually got to the stage by then that although waters were getting sought after, there was little interest shown in the smaller gravel pits the major gravel companies were digging. There was a lot of test digging that was overlooked, especially around the Surrey and Middlesex areas, with the massive network of motorways that were springing up almost overnight. The search for gravel was forever being extended and these small test pits were all over the place. They really were of little or no use to the gravel companies on a commercial basis so they generally either sold them, or they let them out to small angling clubs and syndicates.

Stuart's was very much one of these waters. It was actually bought by a private owner who did not fish and he in turn decided he would let it out on a limited syndicate basis. At the time we were probably paying out

£50 or £60, I can't remember the exact amount of money, but it was certainly under £100. There were waters certainly that were starting to reach the £100 per year money range and as we now know, have well exceeded that.

I tended to fish the little syndicate water at weekends and, at the very most, we might have found there were three people down there. You could move around, that was the nice thing. It was very much a semi stalking situation. There was, I think, only about eight swims on the lake. One bank you couldn't fish as there were private houses there, so we had just the one bank to which we had access. Most of the fish were caught under that far bank at the bottom of these people's gardens. This was the sort of water that had almost been forgotten. Basic tactics would still catch fish here. There were one or two lads who had not even resorted to boilies, let alone the hair rig!

Naturally, as you know, I like to capitalise on situations and I used the hair rig with boilies but not in any way to hammer the place. It was just a nice little place; we had a caravan there – a loo even, which was really quite something. This was a complete change, we were able to stop fishing and have a brew up and I could actually take the wife down there, so this was very much a social type of fishing as opposed to an out and out just trying to catch very big carp. It was pleasant fishing, nice surroundings with a nice bunch of guys. There was no competition, it was like recharging my batteries after the hectic season at Savay and fishing hard at Longfield. I suppose you get yourself into a situation; I certainly fell foul of it, when you have pressures imposed on you from the outside that you don't really want. I never wanted to catch twenty twenties in a season, fifty twenties in a season, or anything like that. You almost get carried along and it's a snowball effect – suddenly you find that you are fishing for numbers, which is a pretty poor state of affairs.

It's the same with baits – I went through the same syndrome as most people have done. I got really hooked on the protein HNV type of bait. I had gone through this situation of actually putting a lot of emphasis on baits, too much perhaps, and there are lots of other things that come into play.

Really, I have come through the baits syndrome and out the other side. There are some very good baits; I do not believe there is an ultimate bait. I strongly believe that good baiting is more important than the bait itself. I'm not opposed to using carbohydrates these days and certainly at Stuart's that's more or less exactly what I would have used. It would be a basic Semolina Gluten bait with quite a strong attractor in it, such as Blueberry, Blue cheese, some Maple combination. The Maple has been

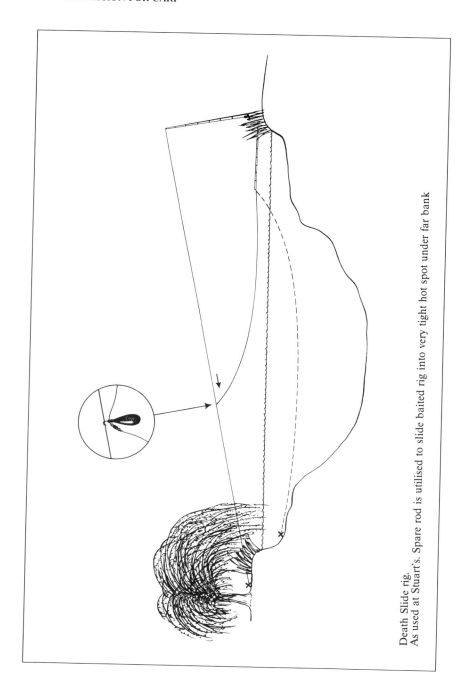

Death Slide rig.
As used at Stuart's. Spare rod is utilised to slide baited rig into very tight hot spot under far bank

such a staggering bait over the years that it has virtually caught me fish everywhere. The Creams and the Butterscotches, all the sweetie type bait. Semolina is such a good carrier for these types of bait. There was no other taste in the bait really other than the attractor, so we tended to keep on the sort of sweetie type of bait and add extra sweetener as well, so it was almost like giving the carp sweeties; they were very palatable baits although they were low in protein.

Lennie Middleton was, undoubtedly, the first person to produce commercial ready-made baits. This happened in 1981 when he actually produced some gelatine boilies. These were moulded baits in a gelatine liquid. The mix was injected into a large mould and converted into solid, set baits. They were the first commercial boilies. Of course, it went on in leaps and bounds after that and Richworth came on the scene and a little later after that, KM Maestro and Crafty Catcher came about.

Boilies were now becoming commercially available and undoubtedly Richworth are the best selling production made boilies. When you look at the ingredients that are included, they are just a carbohydrate bait. I'd certainly like a penny for every carp that has been caught on a Tutti Frutti Richworth!

I probably belonged to Stuart's for about three seasons and I had caught, I believe, all the fish in there, some of them a number of times. There were only half a dozen or so different twenties. They had some pretty fish in there and it was just a nice place to be. I didn't fish it that hard and it wasn't every weekend. It was a now and again fishery and is was more social than anything else. It was nice to get away from it all, it really was. Even today, I am really no longer prepared, or want, to fish the heavily fished waters as they just hold no appeal for me. I guess I would like to sit on some of these places and catch the very large carp, but not alongside hundreds of other anglers. Many of them are now full time anglers.

I enjoy the one to one – myself against the carp. I really don't want to have to compete for the swims – as it has become on most of the waters. Now I am just not interested, so I'm always on the lookout for new quiet waters to get away from it all. Whilst I was on Stuarts there was another water that held a big interest for me which I actually found whilst I was on Savay. Rod Hutchinson introduced me to a Colne Valley water which was then called Pit 4. It had a number of other names; I think it was called the 'Angling Times Pit' at one stage, and it ended up as 'Pit 4'. This was a GLC water and it was in a peculiar situation of first come, first served. When you sent your money to the GLC there was no guarantee that you would get a ticket. Sometimes you received a ticket and other times you didn't, but at the time there were very few people fishing there at all.

It was another of these very quiet little waters, fairly unknown. There had been carp caught from there at 20lb plus and it was another water away from the madding crowd water where I put in a fair bit of time. I actually put a fair bit of effort into Pit 4 because it looked as if it was really going to produce the goods. It did eventually, but not while I was there. I had fish to the upper twenties and it was, I believe, the next year that it produced its first thirty, but it looked like going on to be another very famous water and, unfortunately, with all the attendant pressure that goes with these waters. When you go to a new lake how you start to tackle it really depends on the pressure that is employed on the lake. If you have got a very naive lake, with no pressure on it, then you can look at all the places you know the carp are going to be – there are almost guarantees. If you take something like a one hundred acre lake, you've probably got six miles of bankside margins. That is quite staggering when you think about it and that is where the carp are going to be for ninety per cent of the time. If there are not a lot of anglers there, then you have got these areas of margins where most of the good fishing is going to be. As the angling pressure increases, they will move away from these marginal areas and find new margins, and these might be by way of distant islands, or submerged bars, or whatever. Carp don't like to wander in empty, featureless areas of the lake, they like to follow specific routes. Once you have actually sussed out how they act in different conditions, this whole mental picture builds up in your mind and it's really not something you can easily explain to anyone.

Over the years you get a certain situation that may develop on a tiny one acre pond somewhere or other which triggers off a reaction. It may be temperature, it may be something to do with pressure. Something clicks in your mind that you have seem this somewhere before and you know the fish are going to be feeding in certain areas of that lake at that moment, given these particular conditions. This really applies whether if is a one hundred acre water – or just one acre. I have never been daunted by the prospect of a big water; in actual fact, I have found big waters somewhat easier than small waters. Generally speaking, there are areas on these very large gravel pits that I would write off immediately, as the carp never seem to visit them on a regular basis. There are areas of some large pits where I'm sure carp are there, certainly on a daily, if not weekly, basis, even when the weather conditions are not that favourable, so they are the places I would look at first.

It's a mental picture that you build up in your mind; you always try to imagine what is underneath the surface. When you look at a blank sheet of water there is no character to it, but if you can get inside it, get under its skin and try to get a feeling of it, you can almost feel where the carp are going to be. They do run along the side of bars like motorways. People can find bars easily just by plumbing around, but there are certain parts of the bars that maybe not everyone is aware of, where the carp are more likely to gather. There may be a slight depression in that bar; there might even be a gap in that bar and they would use this almost as a passing point. They don't particularly like to rise high in the water to go over bars; if there is a depression in the bar, or a gap, they are more likely to go through that, so you can actually get the lake population assessed, even if it is one hundred acres being funnelled through an area that is not more than four feet wide!

You can buy rods, you can buy bait and you can use the latest rigs but you can't buy watercraft or the experience of time; they are things you are born with, or acquire. There are anglers who have almost what is a sixth sense, an instinct to know where carp are. I suppose it is something you may learn by observation over many years, but it doesn't come easily. There are certainly lucky anglers; luck will always play a part in angling – not a great part, but it will play a part.

Confidence is undoubtedly the biggest factor and this only comes with experience. It is a peculiar thing and it's something that is very difficult to explain. We all get feelings – or those of us who have been carping for a long time do – and even when weather conditions scream at you, our instincts can hold us back. For example, there might be a north wind blowing and you really should be down the southerly end of the lake because you think they may be stacked up there like breeze blocks, but something inside you suddenly tells you – no, they are going to be somewhere else.

This worked on Pit 4, it really did. There were areas of the lake that people – well, in fairness, there were not many people there, but the few anglers who were fishing – totally ignored. I always try to look for holding areas; most lakes have these. Carp love to sit in trees, I am sure they feel safe in them; if there are submerged trees in the water they will always be there.

Generally, anglers don't like these areas because they are fairly hard to fish. They are not very accessible and they cannot set up their bivvies. There will also be feeding areas and places where the carp are en route to and from these other areas, so there are always lots of opportunities to intercept carp whether they are actually sitting in a holding area, feeding, or en route. There are loads of these areas on Pit 4.

Of course, the other beauty about carp, which is not quite so true with a lot of other fish, is that they show well. You know they jump out of the water and head and shoulder; they bubble and they lie on the surface and they are big lumps of fish. It is not like trying to look for an 8oz dace in a big area of river, a twenty pound carp is a big lump of meat swimming about in the water. Keep your eyes open and your wits about you and they are not that difficult to find. Even half a dozen fish in one hundred acres, on occasions, will be fairly easy to locate.

I had lots of twenties from Kingfisher lake. In actual fact they were virtually all twenties; they were generally lightly scaled mirrors to leathers. Most of the fish were between twenty and twenty five pounds. There were a few upper twenties, but generally they were in this bracket. I had a few multiple catches there; I had five twenties in a short session there. I would go two or three times and not catch a fish, but would always learn a little bit more. It would become even more predictable every time and you built up this store of knowledge and eventually it all clicked into place and you capitalised on the situation.

Baiting was another key. It's something I have always given a great deal of attention to. Many anglers specialise in rigs or rods or anything else. If anything, over the years I suppose I have specialised in the actual

One of the few commons from Kingfisher Lake

baiting of the lake, not the bait itself – I don't pay too much attention to that. It has got to be a good bait, but more important, is the amount of bait you put in, how much the carp will eat, and where you bait up. I try to swing everything in my favour. If I can actually get a bait going into the water that the carp can almost get preoccupied on, then really, a lot of these sophisticated rigs and the distance casting, go out of the window.

If there is competition for food, when you've got carp on the bait the sophisticated set ups really don't mean anything at all. When you have only a few baits out, even if there are large numbers of carp around, you are only giving yourself the opportunity to catch one carp. If you only have four or five freebies or maybe up to fifty freebies around each hookbait, that rig then tends to have to be far more sophisticated than that of the angler who's fishing with several thousand baits. Where the carp are there in numbers, there may be a dozen or twenty carp, all feeding on thousands of baits, in competition with each other, and that hookbait is not going to be as closely inspected by the carp as the one belonging to the guy fishing with a few freebies round his more sophisticated set up. So there you have two trains of thought. Of course, if everything goes full circle, I wouldn't advocate heavy baiting programmes on all waters. There are waters that I would fish with hookbaits only and some where I would fish with only stringers. They have seen it all and they shy off heavily baited areas, but I try to keep to the waters where this baiting programme does work and it has been very successful for me over the years on numbers of waters.

During the 80's carbon fibre had really started taking off for carp rods. I believe it was the Kevin Maddocks' rods that were the first commercially available made on carbon fibre blanks. I'd been using the fibre glass 'Cloopers' up until that time. Because we had gone for more advanced materials with the carbon fibre being lower in diameter and lighter, we were now seeing a trend towards twelve foot rods as opposed to the ten and eleven foot rods that we had previously been using. With these new materials it was now possible for us to cast the same sort of distance as we were fishing, but we could use much heavier tackle. Where we were going down on five and six pound lines with the 'Cloopers' and shock leaders to cast eighty or ninety yards, with these lighter rods that cut through the air that much easier and are also a little bit longer, this extra foot gives you quite a bit of distance.

We were able to use 8lb line straight the way through with a 2oz lead, and easily cast eighty or ninety yards. It was no longer a problem. The biggest obstacle of course was getting your freebies out that distance and it was about that time that the very strong Latex started to become available. Before, we were using natural rubber, square or round sections on a catapult, which was fairly restrictive. With the new Latex and the hunting type catapults coming in from America, which were designed for shooting ball bearings at vermin, baiting up at long range was made easier. On the right day, given the right conditions, you could actually catapult three quarter inch diameter boilies in excess of one hundred yards, which was unheard of before. This, therefore, opened out some of the distant margins where the carp had now been pushed and this was quite a major development.

Hooks – we had been fairly limited on hooks up until the 80's. There were Jack Hiltons and Richard Walkers. We used low water salmons and Au Lion d'Ors, but now there was a new breed of hooks starting to become available that were aimed at the carp angler. It had always been a gripe in the past that there were no hooks suitable for carp fishing but now there were – not many, but there were a few; a new breed of hooks coming along, much shorter in the shank, much wider in the gape. These really were ideal for using with a hair rig because when you look at most of the early commercial hooks they were all wrong for hair rig fishing, they were very long in the shank and very narrow in the gape. Now we were looking to try to expose more of the hook to the carp. This was another major step forward and we had the likes of Partridge and Mustad to thank for starting something of a revolution in hook manufacturing. At long last someone was listening to the needs of the angler.

10 — Burton
Dream-maker, Heartbreaker

Chris Ball and Jan Wenczka started fishing Frensham, the water that was code-named Burton, while I was still living at Tooting; I went down there and had a look around. We were having this constant communication and up came the story about these lovely great Leney fish that were in there. Everyone knows about Burton now, but it was kept fairly close to people's chests at the time.

In actual fact, the name Burton came about by one of Stevie Neville's sayings – because of the goings on there he called it Burton-on-Sea. It is on National Trust property, though it's not a Leisure Park as such, but it's somewhere that people will go and spend a Sunday afternoon when the weather is nice, because it has got very beachy areas. Very shallow, lovely to go and have a swim in, it is not unusual to see several hundred bathers round there on a good day. You could arrive there on a nice, sunny day and be faced with difficulty in getting a swim – not by anglers, but just by bathers everywhere!

I don't know the actual acreage of it, but certainly no more than about thirty five acres top whack. It is a peculiar shaped water. You can't fish it all; the water level goes up and down and, because it's shallow and lies in lowland, the actual acreage is constantly changing.

The name of the lake is actually Frensham Little Pond. The biggest problem is that during the Second World War, because there are two ponds at Frensham, they were an absolutely ideal night siting for German bombers coming into that area. It was obviously army orientated land (near Aldershot) and a very good target for the Germans. What the authorities decided to do was to dewater the small Frensham and try to disguise its presence – on a map it would be two great areas of water, empty one and you would confuse the Germans no end. That was fine and as you can imagine, with a mature water like that, the life sprang up overnight so the result was a large, drained piece of land which was very fertile. Pine trees started to spring up left, right and centre over the ruddy thing.

Once the war ended it had to be reflooded and restored to its normal condition. A contract was given to a local firm to remove all the bushes and trees that had grown up. Now, their idea of tree removing wasn't quite what you and I might think is right – they chopped them all off so there were two foot stumps all over the place. That was quite handy in some respects, but when they reflooded it we now had an underwater jungle with little stumps.

It's a beautiful lake, quite open, very reedy and shallow with lots of beachy areas. They put these wonderful Leney carp in there in 1951. They were the fast growing strain, very long, slender fish. There were lots of linears, commons, and even a few fully scaled fish. They were growing to quite substantial sizes. In actual fact there had been an upper thirty out, so I really had the bit between my teeth; Leneys are my favourite strain of carp, they really do look the business.

It had been fished for many years prior to Chris fishing it in 82/83; there were a couple of Portsmouth lads and they fished it for many years; people like Dennis Smale, Richard Lloyd and Paul Harris did quite well on there. They had all caught quite a lot of fish there, but it was a small band of anglers who had kept things to themselves.

Gradually the word started getting around and Chris was very interested – and so was I. We had a few walks round there and I wanted to have

An early 1984 Burton picture

a go. The distance involved made it a bit prohibitive for me, so Chris actually did a season on there before I managed to fish the place. Chris teamed up with Jan Wenczka and Terry Glebioska and they did extremely well. Chris and Jan both had a thirty pounder out, which was quite something. These fish were taken about sixty to seventy yards out; because of the shallow water you could wade out in ordinary thigh waders and give it the big heave-ho to get well out from the bank.

Because there was a lot of activity around, the fish were generally pushed out towards the centre of the lake. As you can imagine, there were a lot of problems. Fishing over seventy yards of little tree stumps is a bit of a headache and the sort of rigs they used didn't help the situation either.

We talked long and hard about baits. It was very silty and I said to Chris that I thought fishing pop ups would be ideal in this sort of situation. In the end, because of the distance casting and the silt, they fished them directly off the lead on quite short links, so they came directly up off the bottom. Probably by the time the lead had gone in the silt, the baits were two or three inches above the lake's bed. They clipped up ever so tight to induce a bolt on a hair rig.

The fish, in this shallow water (three to four feet at most), would pick

A Burton fish

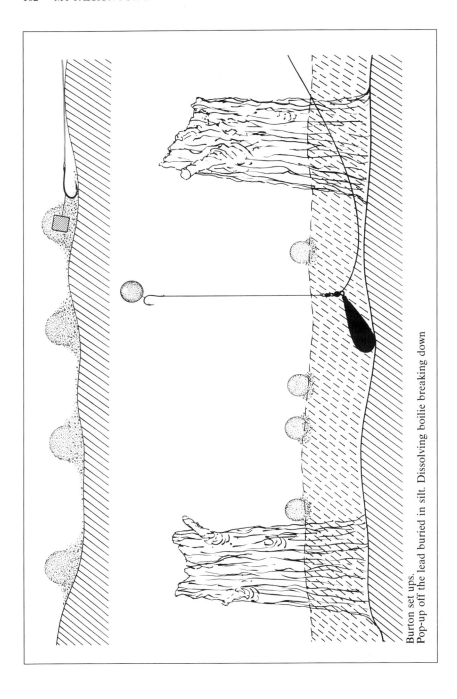

Burton set ups.
Pop-up off the lead buried in silt. Dissolving boilie breaking down

up the bait, hook themselves and really scream off. Well, they only had to move two feet and they were round a snag, so there were more fish lost than put on the bank. It was a hell of a problem. However, they did land some of these lovely carp and I couldn't wait to get there.

It was the next season when I finally had my first session there. That is one I shall never, ever forget. Chris said the only reason he had brought me along was to sort it all out, but that was the last thing I did – I made a complete hash of the whole thing!

I didn't rely on Chris and Jan's advice – I always like to see them at first hand. I've only ever been caught out once and I had no intention of being caught out again. Obviously the fish had been caught, because I had seen them, but I still wanted to go and look for myself. There are areas you can't fish there, such as the lily pad bay behind the warden's house – this is a very good vantage point to go and see them. In addition there is a bird sanctuary area that you can't fish.

I tried to get in to have a look when they were spawning; at Burton they always showed themselves. You could actually sit down there, early in the morning and fish would crash out all over the place. One nice thing about it was that when the water was low you could almost walk right across it, just put on a pair of swimming trunks and the water only came up to your chest in most places. What we tried to do was to get down and actually do a bit of prebaiting, and watch at the same time. Probably one or two evenings a week I would go there and a couple of early mornings as well. We put some bait in and watched to see the fish's reaction to it.

I decided to use a bird seed bait. The previous year, Chris had gone in with cheese flavour and sweetener. I thought something different had to be used and I really fancied using a bird seed mix which had been very successful for me. On this sort of water these types of bait break down very quickly. Once the bait broke down what you were left with was a lot of crustaceans, hemp and other seeds all over the bottom. So rather than the bed of bait being large boilies, it all broke down and became part of the surface layers of silt. As the fish were digging around for bloodworm and everything else, they got a taste of the bait, so it was a very good way of weaning them on to it and we baited quite extensively. We did put some in!

Usually we would put in very large baits to avoid the tench. These would hold together for something like twenty four hours. If carp didn't take them in this period, they would start to break down and what the tench didn't clear up would be left to become part of the silty bottom. We put in several hundred two inch diameter boilies every week, so we really did expect it to go well. In actual fact we saw them taking baits in the lily pad pool. It was a known good bait, one I had caught a lot of fish on; I was pretty sure it had not been used before at Burton. Once we weaned the fish on to these we thought we would have it away because I feel that if carp will take a bait on one water, they will take it on another. There are certain baits that stand head and shoulders above the others. When you look up and down the country at all the baits people use, the top dozen are very similar – you'd be surprised!

The rig was virtually the same as they had used the year before: there wasn't much opportunity to vary it. The only difference I made was to use running, rather than fixed, leads.

The idea behind using fixed leads was that the lead would go along with the running fish – so that the lead was close to the carp and wouldn't get caught up in the snags. That was nice in theory but it didn't turn out that way.

My idea was to use a free running lead, or even for a lead to fall off on a weak link. It just didn't work out, I don't know why. We had no trouble getting takes, they were completely on the bait.

I shall never forget that first night. We all got down fairly close together. Chris set up on one end of the beach where he had had his

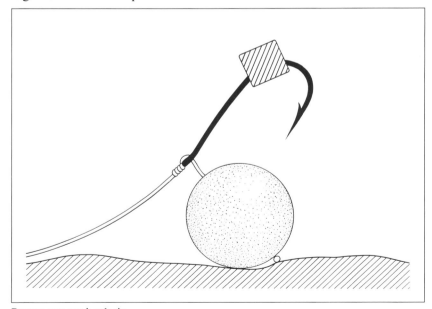

Burton pop-up hook rig

terrific catch – a thirty and two twenties. I chose the opposite end of the beach.

Jan came down several hours later and doubled up with me, so that we could fish the same swim. As luck would have it, we had put ourselves in the snaggiest area of the lake. What happened was that I was baiting at long range, wading out, and then casting out another eighty yards or so. I would guess we were fishing at one hundred yards plus. Rods were quite high, clipped up again because we wanted the carp to hook themselves.

I managed to lose every single fish I hooked. They went round snags and that was it, you could kiss them goodbye. So I'd failed miserably in what Chris had actually brought me in to do! Most of the others had caught before I got one on the bank. I think during the first few sessions I had over a dozen takes, and it was the fourteenth before I landed a carp! On a lake which only had thirty or forty fish in it, I had already lost thirteen, so I wasn't very pleased with myself at all!

It was soul destroying work – getting a bait and rig right and then losing them. They really wanted the bait, without any doubt at all. Most of my sessions were a day and a night and I had takes every time – I just couldn't put the blooming things on the bank. Something had to be sorted out.

Jan did catch on the opening night. I couldn't believe it and I'll never forget it. Jan is an artist by trade and he'd had a really rough day at work. He'd been in the studio most of the day and was absolutely cream crackered and really, I suppose the last thing he should have been doing was go fishing, he should have been kipping. He got his baits out – I had already lost a couple by then and was well cheesed off. The sort of tackle Jan uses, you don't cast very far; it was quite heavy gear. I think he was about fifty yards or so out, not much further than I was wading.

In the early hours of the morning, crack! He's away, reel spinning like mad – Jan's still asleep! I ran across and rattled his bed chair. He came flying out – I guess the fish had already gone some considerable distance. He bent into it and I will always remember him disappearing into the water. Because it's so shallow, you have to wade out to net the fish. It had gone round a reed bed and was out of sight. I got myself together, pulled my waders on, grabbed the landing net and followed him out. He had the carp under control, bullied it a bit and in it went. It was twenty nine pounds odd, so the first one I saw on the bank was almost thirty pounds – incredible!

That was a lesson really driven home to me, that it was all very well fishing at one hundred yards plus, but you were over a hundred yards of snags. You had a much better chance of landing them if you weren't out such a distance; each yard out increased your percentage chance of losing them.

It was a problem; I really had geared myself up to fish at long range. The fish had been pushed away from the bank, firstly by the shallow water and, secondly, by the activity of the general public. It's bedlam there sometimes I can tell you; on a Sunday it's like Southend beach on a bad day – so many people, you wouldn't believe it! I had decided in advance to fish that spot and, looking back, I think it was a mistake. Another plan of action had to be thought of and jolly quickly.

Firstly, I decided to get away from the beach area because it was the most populated place on the lake. If anyone was going to come down to sunbathe or swim, it would be there, so I moved to an area dead opposite. It was a heavily reeded area and it only had three or four swims. It was in one called the 'Perch' swim that I decided to have a go.

The biggest problem was, that being under the control of the National Trust, they dictated exactly where you could fish. They placed the swims and actually it was quite nice. You had to put your rods right out in the water; they cut slots between the long reedbeds and you had to be many yards from the rods if you wanted a kip or a sit down.

Again, fishing amongst these snags you didn't want the fish to get too far away before you had control over them. If that wasn't bad enough, there were also buoys to protect the bird sanctuary from boats which had lost their way. They were a foot to eighteen inches in diameter, with big wire ropes and concrete blocks on them – so if the trees didn't get you, these buggers would!

Eventually things did start to go my way a bit and I scored. I was standing over my rods in the Perch swim and fish were crashing all over the baits. I had no indicators on because of the depth of the water; I was clipped up solid. The line screamed off and the reel was churning like a good 'un. I hit into this fish and it kited round. I kept it on the top, really winding into it, guided it between the buoys and it went straight in the landing net. Goodness, it was like the weight of the world had been lifted off my shoulders! All those takes and I had finally put one on the bank – and what a cracking fish it was. Twenty minutes later I had another, so I had a brace of twenties. I whizzed round and got Chris and he did the business with the camera.

It all started to come together after that. We increased our baiting up and really got amongst them. Some magnificent catches started occurring – two or three twenties in a session sometimes.

I think this change of fortune was due to a change of area really; doing the most logical thing in the world I suppose. Before, I was fishing at one hundred yards over snags, now it was thirty, forty or fifty yards top whack. We baited up heavily where the public didn't go so much and drew fish into an area which was nowhere near as snaggy as the previous areas. The fish stayed there, they wanted the bait so we got it going in regularly as clockwork and they stayed in the area, mopping this bait up. It was fantastic. The losses were cut down a lot; I was landing about seventy five per cent of what I hooked.

Takes at night were a problem. Invariably you would be on your bedchair, maybe as much as fifteen or twenty yards from your rods and then you would have to get your waders on and run out into the lake to get to your rods. Of course, in that time the carp could have gone a considerable distance. If you were going to lose a fish, generally it was then. During the daytime you would stand out in the water over your rods.

When we approached Burton we were pretty sure we knew what was in there and, subsequently, so it proved. I think at that particular time there was probably three or four thirties in there and something like thirty to forty twenties. Quite good stocks really.

Although it was a fairly large, shallow water, quite rich, they had done well over the years. Your general run of the mill fish was twenty five plus. Quality, rather than quantity. Fabulous fish, fish which are for me, and I'm sure for many others, the ultimate in carp fishing. These great big fat leathers are fine for your pounds and ounces but Leney carp are pristine. 'Real' carp; dramatic looking fish, quite spectacular. Long, lean things, huge great paddles for tails and beautiful scale patterns. Very often deep chestnut in colour and they scrap like hell in shallow water – they really do go a bit, as you can imagine.

June and July was a disaster to be honest. It was much later before we got it together, I suppose in August and September it was the best. It really was super. However, come August time, especially Bank Holiday weekend, we had a few problems then, for not only did we get swimmers in the daytime, we also got them at night. I'll never forget a session there; I believe it was on one of Chris' baits. He was sitting behind some rods and crack! Away it went. However, it was a slow take; we had never had a slow one before so it was really peculiar, it wasn't even tenchy – it was breamy, if anything. In actual fact it was a girly take! One of the moonlight dippers had picked up his bait and was subsequently landed – very nice as well! Not hooked, she had actually picked up the line, thank goodness. There were all these sort of problems, as you can imagine. These young things coming down after a party and going skinny dipping. It was quite entertaining to say the least.

Between us, I suppose we'd had about twenty fish by now. The majority all over twenty – very few under twenty. Still no thirties to us yet.

My first thirty from there came in a brace of thirties on an early morning session. Chris and I had decided to meet down there: we'd had a lot of fish from this reeded area and we had started to push them out. We'd had such a successful time that, in actual fact, they had moved.

We decided to fish another area at the opposite end of the lake and we would do a recce one morning, stick a bit of bait in and see if we could find them. It was one of those typical misty mornings around September, quite cold in fact. We sat there and there was no action at all. It was very still and we didn't see any fish move at all. Chris said he was going to call it a day and get off to work. I decided to give it a couple more hours and I decided to move. As I stood up to wish Chris goodbye, I was sure I heard a fish crash out several hundred yards down the lake. I told Chris that I was going to move, give it a couple more hours then go off to work myself.

I picked up the rods, walked along the bank and got within yards of where I though I'd heard the carp and another one poked its head out. It

An amazing mirror caught after a long cast

was an area I hadn't fished before. I put a bait out there and I hadn't even got my second rod out when, crack! The first one went away; the fish gave a tremendous tussle as well. Now this was an area which was very snaggy, it was probably the second most snaggy area in the lake. The lead got caught round a snag but the line carried on running okay. All I could do was bring it back to the same place; so I stripped off and, God, it was cold! I paddled out there, up to my chest in water, felt down and cleared the line from the snags then it was round another and another and so on. By now I was a hundred yards down the lake and I was still attached to this carp. Finally it got free. I grabbed the landing net and put it under what was to be our first thirty pounder. I believe it went 31lb 4oz and it was a really tremendous looking fish – it really was fantastic. Very long, I would guess about thirty one to thirty two inches from nose to the fork of the tail. Quite a heavy scaled fish, a really pretty fish.

I looked round at this place, which is normally packed with people, and no one was around at all. I thought Chris couldn't have got very far so I quickly sacked it up and, just in my underpants, I ran round to the car park to see if he was still there. However, he had gone. I came back to dry off and get myself together. I thought there was bound to be a dog walker or someone coming round so I just left it sacked for a while. Well, no one came round for half an hour or so and I decided to put the baits out while I was waiting, in exactly the same spot, bearing in mind I had actually been paddling out there. Blow me down, I was away again!

Now there hadn't been any freebies at all. Again, a mirror image of the last fight and I had to strip off again. By now my teeth were chattering ten to the dozen. In the net again and she went 30lb 10oz. A brace of them.

Fortunately, a dog walker did come along and I got a shot of a brace of thirty pounders together. I bet he wondered what this lunatic was up to, paddling about in his underpants! Even better, the shots came out as well. On the phone to Chris that evening, he just couldn't believe it. We'd have bet that nobody was going to catch that day so it was really special.

I pulled off shortly after that; it started to get a bit difficult so I went back to Cutt Mill and had a few sessions there. I don't know what it was, but as it was getting into winter I had an inkling that I should be back at Burton again. No one had been fishing it for quite some time; everyone had pulled off. I had returned for a couple of looks and it looked horrible. The water had come up by now, it was really cold and I really didn't fancy paddling about in it, but it just felt right. The reeds had died down, hardly anybody was about.

One evening after work I felt I should be down there. I went back to the swim where we'd had the most success, down in the reedy area. I didn't fancy paddling about on the beach because we were up to chest waders by now. The water had come up and acreage had increased.

I went down to our little 'secret' swim, as we called it. We only had to fish at thirty yards or so. I wondered what on earth I was doing out there; it was a cold night and there was a strong wind blowing.

I put some baits out, the same as we had used all season. I catapulted a few freebies out, put rods on their rests and got back to the bank as soon as possible because I was jolly cold. I took my waders off, put my Moon boots on and sat in the darkness thinking, 'this is absolute madness' – there wasn't another person around and it was a very inhospitable place in the winter. It was quite open, the wind howled and I got really cold.

I think it must have been somewhere around 8 o'clock when one screamed off and frightened the life out of me. Of course, the Moon boots had to come off, I had to get my chest waders back on and paddle out to the rods. The reel was an absolute blur when I reached it. I hit into the fish and it had probably gone another thirty yards or so. Another tremendous tussle with the fish, up and down, all over the place. Eventually it went over the net and, blow me, if it wasn't a 20lb common. I couldn't believe it; first fish back and what a cracker! Here I was, out on my own. I knew I had to get someone, so I sacked the fish up, pulled the other rod in and raced off to the phone box. Chris was out, so Stevie Neville came down and took some photos for me. Of course, as soon as I could, I got back on the phone to Chris and told him 'It's all on mate. They are there' – because I'd heard others crash out and they were still in that spot.

The next session, we went down and it was incredible what happened. Jan, Chris and I all turned up together so we all fished around this area. I suppose it was an area twenty five yards square that we covered with six baits between us. There wasn't enough room for us all to fish one side, so Jan and I fished the area where I'd had the common from and Chris went round opposite us. It was a considerable walk round, but across the water it was no distance at all, so we had baits very close together.

Jan was away first, for he had a take just on dusk. I waded out to net it and it was a cracking twenty six pounder, a lovely fish; absolutely pristine in its winter colours. We thought, 'This is it, we have really cracked it'. We photographed it and put it back.

Chris had pulled his rods in and come all the way round. I would guess it would be the best part of half a mile he trudged round. Moon boots, thermals, the lot – you can imagine how the poor old lad felt! He shook Jan's hand and said he was off back again to cast out, so off he trotted – all the way round again! Cast out, he hadn't been round there two minutes and Jan was away again, would you believe? Another screaming take so I rushed off to help with the netting in the water. I was out there and I could see this fish wallowing about, when, all of a sudden, mine went. I thought Jan's carp must have caught my line with us fishing so close together so I didn't take too much notice of it. Chris was yelling out, 'Hit that bloody take'.

'No, no Chris – it's only a liner, don't worry old boy'.

Trouble was, Jan's fish was nearly in the net and my take was still going. Five seconds later, the penny dropped and I did a very silly thing. Instead of getting out of the water and running round the bank, I actually tried to run through four feet of water! You can't do that very easily, so I ended up with more water in my chest waders than outside them!

I finally got to the rod, only to find that two hundred yards of line had gone and it was right down to the spool knot. Somehow or other I managed to retrieve it. I looked across and saw a fish in the half light, crash right in the reed bed on the other side. I thought, 'oh no, if that's mine I have no chance!'

Meanwhile, poor old Jan was struggling with his carp. By this time Chris had reeled in again and was by my side. It was like we needed a respirator between the two of us. I was totally knackered from struggling through the water and Chris was in a similar sort of condition, having run all the way round three times by now. I had to pump this two hundred yards of line back on to the reel. Believe it or not, somehow or other this fish had gone round two buoys and umpteen snags, but on the way back it avoided them all. In the net I'd got a twenty pounder, so it was getting better and better. Three fish on the bank in under an hour.

Chris had to go back round yet again. All six baits went out again. I really didn't expect any more takes; I went over to chat to Jan and have a cup of coffee. Blow me, mine went off again. Unfortunately, I lost it. In actual fact it didn't snag me, the hook pulled out but I don't think Chris had any energy left to walk round again.

He did get a take at long last! You could hear it sing out; we heard him paddle out to his rods and strike. We expected to be shouted at any moment but it went very quiet. We yelled across to him to ask if he needed any help.

'No, I've got it on the bank. It's a bloody chub'.

The only chub in the lake and Bally had caught it!

In fact, things didn't go his way that winter at all. I don't think he got one in the end.

Jan and I really did do it between us. We caught a lot of fish. The next session Jan had a twenty six and a thirty at the same time, so it was a fabulous winter.

None of the other anglers bothered with the water. Certainly in winter we didn't see anyone at all, there was just the three of us. It was super, especially as it was my first season on there. Lots of big twenties, two thirties. Jan's thirty was just fabulous fishing, they were all pretty fish as well.

We were still keeping it to ourselves, we didn't broadcast it to anyone but because we did catch a lot of fish, it was there for people to see. There was a bunch of lads and a couple of them had wandered round when I had one in the night, to have a chin wag. I had a screaming take, a real flyer, bent into it and one of the lads offered to net it for me. We netted it two hundred yards down the lake; it rolled over in the net and I guess it was twenty eight plus. Very long, lean fish. Yet we never saw those lads again – amazing. So people did know of it.

I ended that season with about twenty seven fish. I'd had a grim start but that was more than made up for by the brilliant finish!

11 — Return to Burton

I don't usually fish more than one year on a water, but I decided to do another season at Burton. Apart from Savay, Burton was one of the few waters to really get to me. Fabulous fish; I had doubled up on a few, for sure, but I wanted more. Chris had adequately documented all the different fish in there and it was certainly in excess of thirty five different twenties. I had only scratched the surface of it so I had to go back. I felt we'd got it together but I knew a lot more could be done.

We decided to go in on the same bait and rig so we used the close season to look at other waters. The Hollybush pits looked good – the water that Chris and I had found – so time was spent looking there. I actually decided to start off the season with Ron Buss at Burton but we nearly didn't bother. It was really hot the first day and I went round to pick up Ron; we loaded the car up and it was full to the seams.

We arrived at the turning to go down to the lake and were stopped by the police. 'Sorry lads, you can't go down there, it's full up'.

However, we did eventually find a bit of grass verge to put the car on and we walked down to the lake. You couldn't actually see the beach – it was completely full of people. The water itself resembled the start of Cowes, there were so many inflatable and rubber dinghies and lilos that you could hardly see the water!

We didn't know what to do; it was getting near dusk and a lot of people were still reluctant to go. Barbecues were being lit. Eventually, we did find a little hole to slot ourselves into and were quite entertained by a few ladies bathing there. Even at midnight it was still crowded would you believe?

We put some baits out and it was rather uneventful because all the commotion had put the carp down. I did, however, hook and lose one at very long range, again on a snag! I was still fairly confident – you can't let all the day trippers get to you! Actually, you had to get your act together to fish the lake at all. Only ten night tickets were available; that way it didn't get overfished. You had to book in advance of course. All those picnickers had put off the long stay carp anglers, which suited us local lads. A few people had cottoned on to the lake's potential, but not many. The lads who were on were a good bunch of guys.

It had changed a bit after the hammering we had given the fish the year before, they had wised up a bit. It wasn't quite the same; I caught fish but not in the same numbers as I had caught them the year before. It was nowhere near as easy, and the fish were reluctant to come close in – so it was back out in the middle of the lake again. The half a dozen regular anglers had all started to don chest waders and even wet suits to put baits out. Sometimes they would walk baits right out into the centre of the lake. Multiple catches dried up; when you got fish it was usually just one at a time. Sometimes you had two chances but usually only landed one. It was back to losing fish again unfortunately, so things had changed quite a bit in a relatively short period of time. Mind you, even though we struggled a bit and fish were all over the place, I knew for sure that come winter I'd really give it a go – and that is how it turned out.

Jan had, of course, taken that magnificent thirty pounder in the winter, so I really thought it was on the cards for another good winter.

Because it fished poorly in the summer and autumn, the lake was virtually empty when I returned early in winter. Back to that same old area, but the fish were not there this time. I did spend a couple of sessions there but when fish showed they did so on the beach area, or way out in the middle of the lake in a very snaggy area. I thought I was going to have lots of problems, because the water was low, unlike the previous winter. We hadn't had much rain so the snags looked even more of a problem. Still, I knew I'd got to fish for them because that's where they were showing.

Believe it or not, that same old bait went out again. I had a couple of takes the first few sessions and lost them both. Chris went and had a go and he also had takes and lost fish. This was getting serious now because we weren't putting any on the bank.

I decided to gun the line up a bit to see if that would do any good. I changed tactics; longer links, running leads, didn't clip up at all. I tried to slow the takes down a bit and get on top of them. Chest waders were the order of the day again to achieve the distance. I was now up to ten pound line so I had to wade out a good thirty yards to be in with a chance of casting to the fish. Eventually, slowly but surely, we started to get them. Chris had the first one, just over twenty pounds, a new fish as well. We were starting to catch again but still having problems losing fish. It was no longer the seventy five per cent success rate we had in the autumn/winter of the previous season; it was now down to less than fifty per cent.

I then managed to catch two on the trot, both twenties. Believe me, I

was grateful for those I can tell you! Then came the one I had really been
looking for. Most fish were caught late afternoon, or just into dark – in
winter that would be 4 – 6 p.m. However, this session I got down quite
early because I wanted to get a bit of bait out in the water. It would be
about 3 in the afternoon; the sun was low in the sky and I saw a couple of
carp head and shoulder over the top of my baits. I put a hookbait
out there.

I had probably been out there for no more than an hour when off it
went. I hooked a fish which felt much better than the couple I had
hooked earlier. It didn't tear off as fast, but it was determined not to give
in. It chugged along; it chugged and chugged and I couldn't manage to
hold it, I had to backwind all the way. It was over one hundred yards out.
It had gone out and kited left about fifty yards so I was well low on line. I
followed it out in chest waders, keeping close to the bank at all times.
Fortunately, a few others were down and I gave one of them a shout. He
brought a net along and after a very long battle up and down that lake, at
last I got it in the net. My God, it was an absolute monster, really staggering; length thirty five and three quarter inches from nose to fork of tail;
30lb 4oz – a huge, long fish which I had never caught before. Jan had
caught it two years previously at 28lb 12oz. Certainly one of the longest

Chest waders accounted for this fine mirror

fish I'd ever had.

I did go on to catch a few more fish but that was the highlight of my winter, as you would expect. That fish was quite something; it was so long you couldn't hold it property, a bit like an eel – more sticks out at either end than fits your hands. Tremendous fish, absolutely huge.

We had been fishing on this beach area which was black at night. Chris had a new toy, which was his video, so every lunker we caught had to be recorded. Trouble was, how the hell do you video something in the middle of the night? Fortunately, we were fairly close to the cars on this beach and we asked the warden for permission to put our cars next to his house. He lives over the water, as part of his house is on stilts above the water, so we could sack fish up literally in his garden. We could bring the cars down, put our headlights on and do our videoing. One evening, when Chris caught a fish, the warden wasn't in and he had to do the videoing on the side of the road where we had parked. He stood there, doing his posing when along came the police and they wanted to know what the hell was going on! Of course, they didn't believe us. 'Videoing carp? You've got to be kidding!'

Chris managed to talk his way out of it, like he always did, and the fish went back. Our two police friends loved every minute of it.

30 plus carp making it onto video

The winter started to close in. Chris and I had got this area sewn up, everyone else had pulled off. Jan hadn't joined us so we had it to ourselves. Unfortunately, Chris lost a very good fish close in, on a snag which we didn't even know was there. Because it was so cold we had to sit in Moon boots. Usually you could net them in Moon boots, but not always. Suddenly, Chris had got this fish jammed in only about two feet six inches of water, three to four rod lengths out, on a snag we didn't know anything about. Unfortunately, he didn't think it was a tree stump, pulled a bit too hard and lost it. The snag turned out to be a log about six feet long, which I only discovered when I waded out to cast, tripped over it and nearly drowned in my chest waders. Luckily, we managed to get it out. Unfortunately, once we had got on these fish, just before Christmas, it started to freeze up and it stayed frozen for quite some time. It wasn't until January that we could get out again. By then, for whatever reason, two or three others had decided to fish as well. People we had never seen before had set up in the swim where we had had all our fish from, so I went round almost opposite to the Perch swim. I tried a long cast across and caught one, which turned out to be a low twenty. That was to be my last ever carp from Burton.

Two sessions after that, on a Sunday afternoon, I was sitting ready for action, when two lads said that a great big pike was dead in the water. I reeled in and went to look at it. In nine to ten inches of water I could see, not a pike, but a dead, twenty pound carp. This was not good news. I looked at the fish, it looked okay. I pulled it out and buried it. I could see seagulls pecking at something wedged in the weed and it didn't take long to put two and two together. Lo and behold, another twenty plus was dead. This was disastrous and so it went on and on, every session produced more dead carp. A very sad occurrence.

Naturally, the Farnham Angling Club, who controlled the water, were very worried. Experts from the Thames Water Authority were brought in but nothing could be found. The carp looked almost perfect when they died. It is very easy to point the finger when something like this happens; it may be coincidence, but just before Christmas there was a stocking of fish that were put into two of the Society's waters and fatalities occurred at both. Perhaps these new carp brought something in with them – who knows? It certainly wasn't intentional for I'm sure the stocking was carried out with the best will in the world and every precaution was taken, but I believe it was a hard lesson and it definitely hammered home to me just how little we know about these wonderful fish that we spend so much time in pursuit of. We take so much out of the sport but put very little back into it.

The situation for me had become very personal. I had fallen in love with Burton and the fabulous Leney carp that resided there. This passion was so strong that I actually moved to within a few miles of the water, just to be close to it. No matter what carp are stocked there and how large they eventually grow to, it will never hold that same magic for me. There are probably no more than six of those original fish left now.

I did return once or twice the following season but it had gone; just bad feelings left. I shall now just have to live with the memories and I will be surprised if I ever cast a line upon those mystical waters again. Truly, the end of a legend.

12 — Surrey Serenade

I had been fishing some other waters as well as Burton. One of them I had been trying to get into for some time was Send, which was run by the Woking Club. In that year, 1983, I actually managed to secure a place there. It was on July 20th that I first fished one of the pits there called Langmans. There were three – Langmans, Sandersons and Cobbitts. Cobbitts was the water where I had caught my first thirty pounder all those years ago when it was on a day ticket and which had now been taken over by the Woking Club. However, it was Langmans that I was interested in, because there was a 30lb common in there as well as a 30lb mirror and there was not a lot of pressure. These were nice waters, very well run and quite difficult to get into, especially if you were a carp angler.

I did a short session on that very first day and it was just for the afternoon and evening. I caught a 16lb mirror very first time out, so I was well pleased with that.

There was this chap there, by the name of Ron Buss, who I had been told was not quite a nice character. He was the Head Bailiff there and he apparently operated it in a bit of a Colditz style. I was told by the other anglers to be very wary of this chap and I hoped there was not going to be any confrontation there. Unfortunately, I was getting to be a little bit of a name in angling and that's something that sometimes works to your advantage and sometimes it works against you. I was told that this would probably work against me at Send!

I'd actually caught the large mirror, which had the horrible nickname of 'Gut Bucket' at 29lb 2oz, on my second attempt there – just a few days after the first session. It was, I think, about four days after that when Ron Buss came along to check my ticket and there was no mistaking this character. He is a large man, to say the least. I don't mean fat, or anything like that, he was just a very big man with long hair. He came along and literally as he got in the swim, up went my indicator. I thought 'Oh crikey, I'm going to be in all sorts of trouble here'.

Lo and behold, it was 'Gut Bucket' again. I had caught the largest fish in the lake twice within a few days.

Ron Buss wasn't the character that they all made him out to be; in actual fact, he was a cracking guy and I think the biggest problem was that he wouldn't stand any nonsense. He lived for his carp fishing and he really put it above and beyond anything else. He wanted the lakes run in the correct manner and he wanted the fish looked after. How bad's that?

Now Langmans was what I call a carp water. It was – if anyone wants to conjure up in their mind what a carp water should look like – Langmans was really it. There were two or three sets of pads, bars all over the place, lovely little bays, islands, big willow trees overhanging the water and it was very pretty. It was just a nice place to be and, of course, there were some lovely carp in there as well. 'Gut Bucket', the big mirror, was certainly a friendly old fish and I think I ended up catching it about seven times in all over a period of two seasons fishing there.

All the fish were caught not necessarily on the same bait but certainly most of them on the same tactics. I would either fish adjacent to the pads, or maybe in them. The margins very rarely got any attention and I caught a lot of fish there and against the side of the island, but it was generally the heavy baiting that worked yet again. At the time I fished Send, there were probably something like eight different twenties and I think I caught seven of them. I'm fairly sure there was only one other big fish that I didn't catch and that was the common. Some of them I caught quite a few times but it was the baiting that made the difference. I was getting bait going in on a regular basis.

I actually used the fish meals on there; I had gone off the semolina, mainly because there seemed to be quite a lot of other anglers using it. I decided to go in there with fish meals and I was using Shrimp Meal, White Fish Meal and, when it was available, Anchovy Meal. Anchovy Meal was a wonderful ingredient when you could buy it – it's just very difficult to obtain. I was using it with a concentrated Shellfish Flavour and it was really doing the business.

Again, it was just a cheap bait. My emphasis has always been on the amount of bait at the right time. I couldn't afford to use the very high nutritional ingredients like Casein, Lactalbumin, Calcium Caseinate in my baits, in the quantity I was using – I just couldn't afford it, so I looked for other alternatives that were equally attractive to the carp.

With the semolina you tended to use that as a carrier and relied solely on the attractant values of the flavours you put in there. Even at that time the fish meals had been around for quite a few years and I'd used them before on other waters with quite good success. Let's face it, Trout Pellets Paste has been catching carp for years. With the fish meal you have got a completely different attractant level; you don't need the very strong synthetic flavours because the fish meals themselves have an attractor value all of their own. Also, they do the fish a little bit more good than just the basic semolina base alone. So it's another good reason for using them. I didn't particularly want to use a sweet bait in there because they were being used by most of the lads fishing the pit. Strawberry and Maple had caught a lot of fish and also Guava, which was another of the Richworth flavours that had been extensively used in the lakes.

If the carp are feeding confidently on your baits they can consume a large amount of bait and I don't think people, even now, have any concept of just what a 20lb carp can pick up. I would be quite happy, where I was fairly well assured that the carp were feeding well on my bait – and probably to the exclusion of everything else – to have at least 8oz to 1lb of bait per carp in the swim. To most people that would sound a silly amount of bait. You might have a situation that in a particular swim there would be two or three 20 pounders and a few doubles swimming about and I might put 10lb of bait out there, which is a lot of bait!

If you look at some of those waters we have talked about – Send, Pit Four and the like – there are other anglers fishing there; they are putting a bit of bait in here and there; they can't all be getting it wrong with location. How on earth do you persuade those carp to feed exclusively on

Twenty-plus common and mirror

your bait? Some would say bait up everywhere, while others would say just stick it in one place. Now, baiting up all over the lake just doesn't work. It's never worked for me; I like to concentrate the bait in one or two particular areas. If I can, I like to have bait there all the time and by that I mean that I will bait up a swim or an area almost daily, or every other day at the very least, so that every time the carp visit that spot, my bait is always there.

First, you find a feeding area, there's no point doing it anywhere, it has to be in an area where the carp are naturally going to. They are either going there to feed, because it's a holding area or they're en route between the two. It's one of these areas that I know carp are going to be naturally. What I try to do then is to create a feeding area with my bait. At first the carp may only come to it once a day, but after a few days of baiting up with a lot of bait the carp will visit the spot more frequently. They've not necessarily cleared all the bait up, but they've had a few baits and they've moved off because it may be a through area. I'm sure they will remember and they will go back to that particular spot again and again if there's always bait there, and so it goes on – and gradually there is a snowball effect that builds the swim up. Whereas one or two carp may have started off feeding in this area, by the second or third day,

Not its largest inhabitant but a cracker

with this constant baiting, you might have ten or fifteen carp. If the baiting is successful, I would expect literally seventy five per cent of the
lake's population to be feeding on my bait. When you create that situation that is when you know you've got it right and you can catch a lot of
carp! Whilst I was on the Send lakes, I was mainly on Langmans, which
was just one of the three lakes there. I was fishing really for two fish and
one was the big old mirror which I had been very successful with and
had caught quite a few times. I'd actually had it up to about 32lb, but
there was this very nice looking common in there that was pushing 30lb.
I'd had the other 20lb commons – I believe that, in all, there were four
20lb commons in there and I'd had three of them, but the big one had
absolutely eluded me. I just could not catch this fish; I had seen it on the
bank when one of the regulars had caught it and it looked fantastic. It
was an upper twenty and it was obviously going to go over thirty at some
stage. I stayed on there until about November trying to catch the fish
before I moved off and fished the adjacent pit called Cobbitts.

In between times, I decided that I would have a crack at Tri-Lakes,
which was a completely different water. This was a day ticket water next
to the Leisure Sport lakes at Yateley. Originally it was just one lake but
has now been made into two with a peninsula driven between two parts
of it. There were a number of big fish in there, including a couple of thirties. A few of my friends had fished there, one being Dave Reekie. He
had caught a 32lb common which was a magnificent fish, so I wanted to
have a crack at that. Also, my mate Jan had his amazing brace from
there – I think he wrote about it in one of the monthlies. It's one of those
lakes that, although it is known about by a lot of people, even today it
doesn't get that much pressure. There are a lot of day ticket anglers there
who fish for the crucians, tench and roach, but because there is no night
fishing it doesn't get that much pressure from the carp angler. There
have been a few people who have given it a go over the years; Terry
Glebioska and Jan Wenczka spent a season on there and both did
amazingly well. They caught, I think, virtually all the big fish. Jan had
caught those two thirties in the one day and it was the larger of the two
thirties, that at the time was about 35lb, and the very large common that
Dave had caught at 32lb, that I was interested in. I kept going back there
but I really struggled on Tri-Lakes.

I think the biggest problem at Tri-Lakes was that there was so much of
the water that you couldn't fish: because it was a day ticket fishery, with
no night fishing, I think there was a strange situation that I hadn't
encountered before, that the carp were spending most of the days in the
areas where you couldn't get at them.

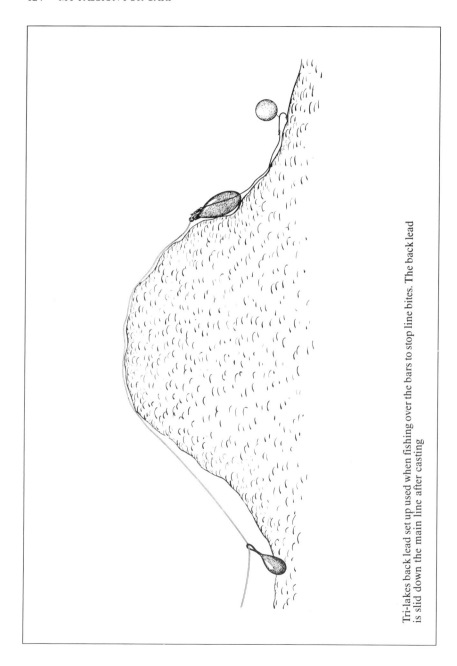

Tri-lakes back lead set up used when fishing over the bars to stop line bites. The back lead is slid down the main line after casting

In amongst this multitude of islands, they were coming out at night and feeding on all the freebies that were left around by the day ticket anglers. You had opportunities very early and very late. You weren't allowed in there until 7.00 a.m. and most of the fish I caught came before 7.15 a.m. After about 7.30 the fish used to seemed to disappear into the islands and often not come out.

Again, it was baiting that did eventually bring them out. There were certain areas that were generally left alone by the other anglers because they weren't quite so accessible – you had to cast between islands and it was all a bit chancy. Eventually, with a bit of baiting and going there every Saturday and one night a week for about 12 weeks, I finally connected with one of the big ones and yes, it was Jan's fish that I had out first. Very much down in weight at 30lb 7oz but I was very pleased with it all the same.

I had been doing a bit of baiting on Cobbitts, which is the one adjacent to Langmans, into the autumn with the idea of fishing there in the winter. There was my old thirty in there, 'Gertie Thirty' as it was known, and there were also other carp in the twenty pound bracket to have a go for.

I also fancied a last crack at the G.L.C. water, Pit 4 over in the Colne Valley, so in November again, I did a bit of baiting up and I alternated between Cobbitts and Pit 4. It really was the start of the winter sessions and I couldn't have had a better start.

I fished at Pit 4 and started catching the fish virtually straight away – the first session back, after a break of all the summer. I had my first 30 out of that particular water and it was a 32lb mirror, which was a cracking fish. I also caught some other twenties there and had a wonderful November. This slipped into December and, for whatever reason, which I can't explain, I decided that enough was enough of Pit 4 and I never went back. I haven't been back since!

It was then that I went on to Cobbitts and had quite a nice winter there really. It was more local to me because I had now actually moved to the Surrey area. I was living at Guildford and, rather than drive down to the Colne Valley every weekend, I now thought that I would fish locally for the rest of the winter. I was doing days only, I didn't bother doing any nights. I fished out the rest of the season on Cobbitts. Funnily enough, I think 'Gertie Thirty' was the only big carp that I didn't catch, which was ironic really, as it had been my first thirty which I had caught all those many years before. I would actually have like to have caught it again, just to renew the old acquaintance. It was that year, unfortunately, that Gertie died, so I didn't catch the fish again, although I saw it on the bank many times.

I had fish up to mid twenties out of Cobbitts and a number of doubles. It was a nice winter, seeing lots of action, hardly ever a blank there. I did most of the Saturdays; I fished it for the whole day and would usually catch two or three fish each time, so it was a pleasant way to spend the winter.

Winter fishing, for some people, seems to have got worse over the last couple of years. The better the weather, the worse the fishing became for many anglers and I think that is the case around the country. I don't know what on earth has happened to our winters, they are not like real winters any more. I would like to return to us having some cold weather because the carp become more predictable. I'm not sure they know what to do with these mild winters we are having; they don't seem to be able to cope with them.

I really love winter carp fishing. I liked it then, around 1983, and I like it now, but it's different. You do have to set the stall out slightly differently and I think you have to put yourself out more. Although at Cobbitts I was only fishing maybe a couple of late evenings and on a Saturday, I would bait up virtually every day.

This was one of the reasons for picking a local water; travelling down to the Colne Valley on a daily basis to bait up was just not on. Financially it was not possible, and time wise it was not practical so for my winter fishing I like to pick waters that I can visit on a daily basis, if not, every other day. I'm a strong believer that it is little and often for baiting up in the winter. Whereas in the summer I'm quite happy to stack in thousands of baits in an area and draw the fish into that area, in the winter carp certainly get into a comfortable area – by that I mean that they do like cover. Where there are bushes in the water, overhanging trees, decaying weed beds, these type of places, they will spend most of their winter in.

Very often, where you can observe the carp, they will be in small groups. There may be four or five fish in an area smaller than a fifty inch umbrella. You have to concentrate on these areas so you are not putting thousands of baits in; more than likely you are only putting tens and twenties of baits in at a time.

Our winters have changed, but even in the colder winters the carp are only ever feeding for a very short period each day, or maybe every two days. If there's loads of bait there every time, you're stacking the odds against yourself because they may only feed for an hour and in that hour they may only pick up ten or fifteen baits. If you put a hundred baits down there, it stands to reason that you've got less of a chance of catch-

ing these fish, unless there are a lot of them there. Therefore, you concentrate on known holding areas, or places where you've actually
worked out for yourself that carp will be there. Presenting baits to them
on a daily basis is enough for them to recharge their batteries. They do
get in this semi-dormant situation, but I don't believe they completely
hibernate. I don't know where the current idea has come from that fish
meals don't work in winter. There have been a number of occasions
when the fish meals have outfished every other bait during the
winter period.

I think it is the anglers who convince themselves of this, because they
have been using the bait all the summer. Let's face it, the fish meals have
had such hype recently – there is not a water round here where fish
meals haven't gone in. They used them all summer and they've been in
quite large quantities with that very high level of flavour and with Fish
Inducing Oils and everything else. Suddenly, because the carp still
aren't being caught in the same numbers during the winter, it's put down
to the bait. Not down to the angler – it's always down to the bait,
which is nonsense.

Actually, I quite like it as it does me a great favour. They have baited
up all summer for me on some of these lakes and then they vacate them
in the winter, because they are no longer producing the goods, I can go
in there, using virtually the same bait that they were using in the summer, trickle it in there during the winter and catch the same old fish! I
just don't pay any attention to this nonsense that fish meals don't catch
carp in the winter.

13 — Oakmere

The 1984 season was a good one for me. We don't very often get them but it was one of those years when everything clicked into place although at first I thought I was going to struggle. I wanted to catch a big carp and by that I didn't mean a twenty or even a thirty – I wanted to catch a really big fish. Not for any other reason than I wanted to catch it. I had earmarked a couple of fish that I really fancied having a crack at.

One of them was on a one hundred acre plus water called Oakmere at Burghfield. It was an extremely difficult water, it very rarely produced carp, but when it did they were generally very large fish. It looked as if I was going to have to spend a great deal of time on there to catch one of them. As it turned out, it was going to be a stalking water, which I never imagined. I really thought I was going to have to do the baiting up routine. I'm sure that at the time there were probably less than twenty five fish in over one hundred acres. In actual fact, there was probably nearer one hundred and fifty acres, so it was a large area of water with only one or two very large carp in it.

During my observations in the close season, I was blessed with nice warm weather. I actually saw what I believe to be the largest carp in there and it looked as if it was probably over forty pounds. It had been caught before and it was a known carp, so I knew the fish I was looking for.

Today, forty pounds is a big fish – it's not a monster because forty pounders are caught today, but in those days it was an absolute monster. It was a staggering fish. I'd had a very large fish out of Longfield a couple of seasons before, which was my personal best and a fish that had actually been out at low forties. I caught it just under forty pounds and this was the first time I had been in front of another fish of that calibre since then, so it was exciting stuff.

The first fish I'd had out of Oakmere was twenty five pounds, which I was chuffed to bits with. I caught that off the top; it was stalked. I had done a very silly thing, the sort of thing most carp anglers will do in their lifetime – and I shall probably do it again – I was very impatient. I got the fish going on the surface and there were a group of half a dozen of them, which was a rarity to find in Oakmere. They were all together, feeding on the surface, and amongst them was the Big One. In haste, I cast, really into nowhere: I didn't particularly try to catch any one of these fish –they were all feeding. I just kept the floaters going out there. This was Felix Meaty Crunch, a cracking bait, which unfortunately is no longer available, which is a disaster. It was a beautiful bait; I caught so many carp on it.

The Big One, although it wasn't taking anywhere near as confidently as the others, was a catchable fish, but in my impatience I just cast out and the first fish that came along was this twenty five pounder. It was a lovely fish but it wasn't the one I was after. I had caught a lot of twenty five pounders so, of course, the rest of the fish went and that was the opportunity gone. Instead, I should have been very patient and selected my fish and maybe had a chance at the Big One. That is what floater fishing is all about – selecting your fish. It's not a lucky dip any more. When you are stalking, whether it is on the bottom, where you can see fish, free lining, slowly sinking baits to them, or fishing on the surface, you can be selective.

These fish were only two rod lengths out, but my impatience got the better of me. I'm not a patient angler at the best of times and it has been my downfall on many occasions. It certainly was on this one.

Oakmere twenty-plus

I caught the first fish from there, which I was excited to catch and then thirty seconds later I was kicking myself because I know I could have done better. I'm sure that probably sounds very mercenary, but it was the way I felt. You set your own targets, you don't fish to anyone else's requirements; if it's a forty you want, then it's a forty you want.

I didn't manage to find that fish for quite some time, the Big One. In between times, I was really chuffed as I did get a thirty off the top. I had a 32lb mirror – I did select this one out. It was with four other fish and it was certainly the largest of these four fish. I was very patient this time for once!

I got them going and I waited until this fish had moved out from the rest. They kept doing this. They would drift out then all split up and eventually come back. I managed to get this one on its own, it was probably ten yards away from the others and I had it feeding on just one or two of those small biscuits on its own. I picked the time just right; it was waddling about and I was able to just drop my bait right on top of it. Down the hatch it went first time and I had this extremely long mirror out, which charged around all over the place – 32lb, so my first thirty out of Oakmere.

Really, that was only the second opportunity I got to catch fish;

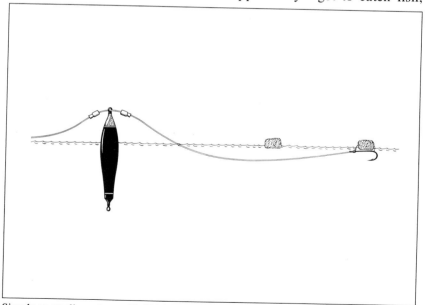

Simple controller set up with 'D' hair rigged floating biscuit, used at Oakmere

although I walked round it a lot, I spent very little time fishing. A lot of hours looking and very little time fishing. I did actually catch another thirty from Oakmere. A low thirty, which was a little, short, fat, dumpy fish and another couple of twenties. It took a long time to find the Big One again; it was a big water and you just had those small pockets of fish here and there.

It was funny, it was another angler who put me on to the big fish again, for which I shall be forever in his debt, for when he came along I was fishing miles away from this fish. He said that he had just seen a very big carp over on the other side of the lake. He described this fish in good detail because the water is very clear there.

I thought, 'Crikey, it sounds like it might be the Big One', so I raced round to the other side and, about two hours later, I actually found the fish. Again it was with the same half a dozen fish, I couldn't believe it!

This time I was determined to get it right and very carefully, I managed to get the carp split up by sort of catapulting a little pouch load to one side and then to the other. Eventually, I got the whole lot of them to spread out and almost roaring around as they went from one group of floaters to another. They were in suicidal form – I knew I had got it right! It was just a matter of time before I got the fish within casting range.

They were out a little bit further this time, about twenty five yards, and eventually the wind turned and was in the right direction. Everything was right, there were no other anglers on the water. Soon they all drifted into this tiny little bay and I was able to walk round and get very close to them. The floaters were blowing into the side of this bay, then within two rod lengths, the Big One came along and out went my floater. I think its co-ordination was diabolical; I was shaking like a leaf because it had about four attempts at taking my bait. It missed every time. I thought I was never going to get a chance with the fish – it kept missing them. It was missing the freebies as well; it knew they were there and it was almost panicking. It was going back on itself trying to get the floaters and eventually he managed to get mine into his mouth. I was quaking in my boots, even from the moment that I hooked it, because it was obviously a monster. This was probably going to be my largest fish and I wasn't going to make any mistakes. I took a long time to land the fish but I could probably have had it in the net in thirty seconds because, in all honesty, it did not fight particularly hard. It is a very fat fish, much shorter than the thirty two pounder that I previously caught from there. Twenty minutes or so later, it was in the net. I was absolutely elated. I was shaking so much I couldn't put it on the scales, so I sacked it up and called a mate. Between us we hoisted it up; at first it looked like it was a forty, but it wasn't and we settled on 39lb 14oz, which was a personal best. I was obviously over the moon with it so it was a good way to start the season. It has since come out at 42lb and that was two seasons ago. There is a little bit of an air of mystery around the water which is great. I love this because it hasn't got a name, which is terrific, and it is one of those waters that a lot of famous anglers have not got on to.

The Sting at 39.14

14 — Plank Island

After that it was really, what the heck did I want to go and do because I had nearly had a forty and I sure wasn't going to better that fish.

It was my mate, Chris Ball, who really came up with the answer. I wanted a bit of fun now – that fish was going to last me for a long time and I just really wanted to go and enjoy myself.

During the close season that I had been looking round Oakmere, we had also been looking at some other waters locally. This was one of the first times that we had been really caught out. We had looked at this little water, Plank Island Pit, dug in the old style, lots of long islands with very thin channels up between. There was no open water as such, you had probably, at the most, twenty five yards of open water in front of you anywhere. A lot of the pits in the forties were dug in this manner and this was a classic example of it. Quite clear. We walked round it and we had a look at these fish. It was a pretty place, no one was fishing there and no one had fished there for several years. I don't know where the fish had come from, but there were a lot of carp in there. There were hundreds of carp, but they all looked very small. We looked at each other, and we didn't really know whether we wanted to fish it, because all the carp looked to be eight or nine pounds. I was fairly keen because there were a few things I wanted to have a go at. I hadn't had an opportunity to really go back to particle fishing for quite a few years. It was really from the Brookland days that I had gone onto boilies. This looked an ideal water for it; it screamed 'particles' at both of us and we thought 'Oh blow it, in for a penny, in for a pound'. We would have a go – and we did, we went in there with tiger nuts. That was the first time I had actually used tiger nuts although they had been around for a long time. We put a lot of tiger nuts in, we had both bought a half hundred weight sack of tiger nuts each. What happened in the next few months was extraordinary.

It is sometimes said that you don't put too much hemp in because they fill up quickly, or you have problems with the fish with a lot of hemp. Well, I think that is absolute rubbish. Hemp comes out the same way as it goes in; it does the carp no good whatsoever. I think it is a brilliant bait for actually putting huge beds down – by huge beds, I mean huge beds. I'd be quite happy to put twenty or thirty pounds of hemp down in a swim, knowing the fish are going to come along. It is going to be a continuous cycle because the faster they eat it, it goes out the other end and gets eaten again. It keeps the carp in the swim and gives you the opportunity of presenting another bait over the top of it. With tiger nuts we were confronted with a couple of hundred carp on this particular pit. They had never seen tiger nuts before and there were large groups of these fish moving around. It was nothing to have maybe twenty or thirty carp coming along in a shoal. They would swim up the side of these little islands – it was great. It was like a massive motorway system for them because they had rows of these long islands and they would just be up and down all the time. We walked all the way round it many times but both Chris and I instantly selected one area. Again, it is this inbuilt instinct; there was nothing particularly different about this spot, but for both of us there was something there that made us decide that this was going to be the spot. It was on the end of one of the little peninsulas and the carp had to come round the end of this island to get into another part of the lake – it just looked a good interception point; it was here that we were going to bait up. We probably put twenty-thirty pounds of tiger nuts down before we fished on the couple of occasions that we went down and had a go. We agreed that we wouldn't fish it together because there wasn't much room. You could only get two rods out in this little swim. It was quite overgrown and there certainly wasn't room to fish there together, so we decided that we would fish it evenings and mornings and maybe alternate. Perhaps I would do mornings one week and Chris do mornings the next week. We didn't fish it for any more than probably six hours at a time. Very often if would only be for two or three hours.

We really did put a lot of tiger nuts in there. What usually happened was that the fish would follow the islands along and they would come to the little spot that we had selected. We were now fishing out about fifteen yards on the edge of this island, in about eighteen inches of water and there would be five or six pounds of tiger nuts there. There would be maybe ten fish there, their heads would go down, their tails would come up and there would be no tiger nuts left. That is exactly as it went so many times. Invariably I would get both indicators going off at the same time – we had so many carp it was ridiculous!

Chris is much better at documenting these things than I am. Looking at his diary for the period from the end of July to the middle of September, we caught ninety nine fish out of there but this was the staggering thing, only one of them was under ten pounds. All those fish that we thought were eight or nine pounds were actually fifteen or sixteen pound fish. We had really got caught out by the size of them; they weren't different fish, they were certainly the same fish we had seen. We actually caught ninety eight doubles between us in that short period of time. There were four twenties amongst them, the largest was 22lb 8oz which Chris caught and I had one at 22lb 4oz, which I believe was the same fish. We had a marvellous time and it was really so different from Oakmere, because I was confronted with a very small area of water with a massive number of fish and no other anglers.

I've got my own way of preparing tiger nuts. There has been a lot written about particles in general, especially tiger nuts. There is very little chance of getting tiger nuts to be very soft. I have heard all these extraordinary preparations that people undertake and they tell me they get them soft. I've never managed to do it. I'm quite happy to soak them for about twelve hours, less when I'm pushed for time. There is hardly any flavour that seems to go into the tigers and stay there, they are not that sort of bait. They have got quite a lot of oil in themselves, so they're an attractor in their own right. I've never found anything that really makes them any better than they are in their natural state. I don't like to boil them, I don't think boiling does them any good at all. I like to pressure cook them; I cook them for twenty minutes. Pressure cooking 50lb of tiger nuts takes a very long time, especially if you are doing a batch of them for twenty minutes at a time, but that's the way we cooked them. Chris and I both prepared them in exactly the same way. They were nice to eat and were still very crispy. They certainly weren't soft by any stretch of the imagination. They could not swell up any more, which I think is the key to a lot of particle preparation. They didn't have to be denatured like a lot of particles have to be. Take chick peas for example; they have to be denatured and there is only the boiling process which will actually do that to them.

Tiger nuts are dehydrated and all you are really interested in is getting them back to their natural size, getting that water content back in there and swelling them up. The soaking for twelve hours and pressure cooking for twenty minutes does that. In fact, I think they end up larger than they would have been in their natural state. So that was the bait, now to the tackle. There were two things that came about in that year. One was chemically sharpened hooks.

I'm sure that Chris Ball and myself were among the first two to use these Japanese chemically sharpened hooks for carp fishing and we were ridiculed for it. Actually, there was a conference where we all sat up on the stage and there was a great debate because it was the thing at the time that chemically sharpened hooks damaged fish and cut their mouths open. A good friend of mine, Pete Springate, actually said he would not use them. He thought they were a bad thing for carp fishing. We now know, of course, that this is just not so, it was a myth. Because they were so much sharper than anything else, people thought that they actually damaged carp. We never lost any carp on them, we never damaged any carp on them and we are still using them today. So that was a bit of a revolution.

The other thing was Dacron, although it had been around for quite some time, especially for sea angling. It was used for deep sea fishing because of its ability to have little stretch, so it was in direct contact with the fish at great depths. It was also very soft, being a braided Terylene polyester. Suddenly, it was the trend to use Dacron for carp fishing.

It was also becoming the vogue to use short hook links. By short, I mean nine inches or less, with heavy fixed or semi-fixed leads of 2oz or more acting as a bolt rig. This was ideal with these very fine chemically sharpened hooks and this is exactly what Chris and myself used. We didn't go to the extent of using 2oz leads, we didn't think it was necessary. We actually used 1oz or 1¼oz with a very short Dacron hook link and size ten or size eight chemically sharpened hooks on a short hair with just one tiger nut on. It goes to show just how preoccupied they were because we would get instantaneous takes as the fish came into the

We just couldn't go wrong, those magical weeks

swim. We might have had five pounds of tiger nuts down there, but our two tiger nuts amongst that lot when a shoal of carp came over the top, would only be there for thirty seconds and we would get a take.

I seem to have this insatiable drive for carp fishing forever. It hasn't left me at the moment, although I do get periods when I'm a bit low and then I don't go – it's as simple as that. There have been periods in my life when I have said I'm not actually enjoying this, and I have not gone carp fishing. I might have gone off and done some other fishing.

I do enjoy it. I wouldn't say it is a way of relaxing, it certainly isn't; I put a great deal of effort into it and I come away shattered on many occasions. I do try very hard; I always try to capitalise on what I've got in front of me. I'm never complacent about the situation, I don't let it happen, I always try to create my chances.

When I return from a session, I'm already planning the next one in my mind. As I'm driving back from an outing and it has not gone my way, I know I've done something wrong. Sometimes it goes right, but invariably that is about five per cent of the time – the rest of the time I know that I could have done better, and I am already planning what I am going to do to make the situation work for me the next time. The rig might not be working quite correctly; I should have put more bait in; I should have moved swims before I spooked all the fish out of there and probably many things I should have done which I didn't. Hindsight is a wonderful thing, it really is and we can all be clever after the event but we have to learn by it. I think it is this thirst for knowledge and progression that has kept me going for all these years.

I suppose I was very fortunate to meet Chris Ball because he has the same enthusiasm that I have for carp fishing. I don't think we will ever tire of catching carp. They don't have to be monsters, we just like to see those indicators going up, or a carp slurp round our floater. It's just there, it's something I can't explain. I really do get pleasure out of carp fishing. I get pleasure out of watching carp and seeing other people catching carp, so that is always going to be there.

15 — Return to the Mill

We had done so well at Plank Islands and we caught so many carp we had started to double up on the fish. I think that is what made us decide that we would give it a rest there and go and look for other waters. I had moved to the Guildford area a couple of years before and certainly, Surrey's most famous water is Cutt Mill, which is run by the Farnham Angling Club (not to be confused with Cuttle Mill which is, of course, the Midlands' most famous carp fishery. It's ironic that their names are so very similar. They are also very similar in the way they produce fish.).

Of course, with this very famous carp water on my doorstep, I had to go and have a look at it. I was told it was a hole in the ground. It has got this air about it that the world and his uncle had fished there. I think virtually every famous carp angler in the world has fished there, or so it would seem.

I just had to go and have a look and I fell in love with the place. I thought it was fabulous, and a pretty water, much smaller than I had imagined it would be. It is in a quiet and picturesque part of Surrey. You can't knock it at all. Yes, the swims were fairly well worn and they have had years of carp fishing. There were a load of carp in there. There were big carp and I could see them. I thought 'I'm going to have a go at this'.

I said to Chris, 'Fancy having a go at Cutt Mill?'

He said 'No, I don't want to know about Cutt Mill'.

He had fished there and had caught his first double there many years before. I think his best one was 18lb during the years he fished the Mill and he didn't want to go back. He just wasn't interested in catching the same fish.

I said, 'Fair enough', and we went our separate ways.

I think he went back to Yateley and I decided that I was going to have a go at Cutt Mill.

I asked around and, of course, 1980-81 had been the year of the Richworth baits going in there. What with the hair rig and the Richworth boilies, Clive and Malcolm took Cutt Mill apart. They took a lot of fish to just under thirty pounds, so it was the trend that followed for the next couple of years. Everyone was using these very sweet, highly flavoured semolina base type baits, so I thought it's no use going along with them as I wasn't going to capitalise on what was in front of me doing the same old thing, I would only catch a percentage of what everybody else was going to catch. I consider myself to be a competitive angler, I always try to better myself; I try to swing things in my favour. That is not to say that I don't enjoy seeing people catch fish, but I do like to try to swing things in my favour. Using the same bait, the same tactics as everyone else certainly is not going to do that for me. I would only bank a share of what everyone else is catching and if you want to catch a large share of the fish, you have got to be prepared to do things off your own back.

So, the old fish meals were resurrected once again. Once more this was a very similar mix to the one I had used before. I managed to get some Anchovy Meal, which was great, and some very good Red Shrimp Meal, so it was back to making up several thousand boilies yet again. I didn't bother flavouring them this time because there had been so many flavours used at Cutt Mill.

I was quite surprised that pop ups hadn't been used too extensively. Considering the amount of pressure that Cutt Mill receives, I did

A nicely scaled big one

assume that it had seen just about every rig that was available.

The current trend there was to use 2oz semi fixed leads clipped up very tightly with the bobbins at the top of the needles on twin bottom baits, which seemed a strange combination to me, but nevertheless, that's what they were using.

I did just about the opposite. I used a fairly short hook link of about nine inches of Biffa braided Terylene, very small hooks and quite small baits. I was down to something like 12mm diameter baits. Considering the size of the baits going in, they were relatively small. Rather than fish with these very heavy leads clipped up tight, I used just the amount of lead that was needed to be cast into the swim, which was about ¾oz. I also left the line very slack in front of the rod tip so that most of the line was actually lying along the bottom.

It's very shallow at Cutt Mill and you get a lot of fish moving between the baited area and your own bank. They were obviously spooking off a lot of these tight lines, so it made sense to use these slack lining techniques. This worked very well with a pop up suspended about four inches from the bottom and straight away I started catching fish.

In fact, the very first session, I remember it was very embarrassing for me. I took the wife and children down there as it's such a lovely place and you can almost park in the swim. We fished on the car park side and I fished just a few yards away from the parked car. With the first take I was away and the fish kited right the way round to the left hand side. As I said, Cutt Mill is very shallow and there are extensive reed beds that go out in front of the swim and I was no longer in contact with the fish. It had gone round in front of the reeds and I had no waders with me. Unknown to me, there was a quite well known angler in the next swim, Johnny Walker with his wife, and they kindly lent me a pair of waders. I paddled out and netted my first fish from the Mill, which I think was about 18lb. I had to borrow the waders five more times that afternoon and ended up with a twenty four pounder – I think that was the best fish. It was a bit like when I fished with Mike Wilson at Savay and had to keep borrowing him for the camera shots. It's nice when people help you out; that is one good thing about fishing. Of course everyone had a bit of a laugh and a joke about it. I was the only one who had come without any waders and they really are essential there, so I spent most of my time wearing Johnny Walker's waders, which was quite something. On my next session I made sure that I had my own waders with me!

Of course, I told Chris and although he said 'Well done, my old mate', he still didn't want to come down there.

I think it was really about the fifth twenty that was turning point for him because for the five twenties, I probably had about forty doubles as well, it was that sort of ratio. I was catching a lot of fish, bearing in mind that I had already had fifty odd doubles out of that ninety odd that Chris and I had caught from Plank Island.

I was up towards a hundred doubles now and it was still quite early in the season. Chris started to weaken a little bit. He came round to look at some photographs and said they were nice fish.

It was planned that the next trip he would actually come down there. It was a horrendous evening and I'll never forget it. It was an after work session and I told him roughly where I would be. I arrived in darkness – this would have been September time. I put the umbrella up and chucked out two rods in the blackness there. The rain was pouring down and Chris turned up and dropped in the swim next to me and asked where he was fishing. I said 'Well, it's sort of out there' – you couldn't see anything and there really wasn't anything to cast out to. Out went his fish meal pop ups and ten minutes later he was playing a fish – after all those years in between catching his very first fish out of the Mill – which weighed 22lb.

A beautiful double row linear – and that was it – he was hooked! I think he's been fishing there on and off ever since.

Cutt Mill's biggy at 28 plus

We had a marvellous time and we caught all the known big fish. I had the famous Leney which was one of the better looking fish in there at 28lb, which was slightly down on its normal weight of 29–29½lb. That fish is another double row linear.

Of course, there has to be a mug. There's a mug fish everywhere and we caught it several times. Twice in one week! I had it on a Tuesday at 27lb 4oz and Chris caught it on a Thursday at 27lb exactly, so it was obviously well on our bait.

All the takes were fairly slow, confident ones. We didn't have any screamers, unless we had a take whilst we were playing another fish that would inevitably prick itself and then roar off at a hundred miles an hour because the waters were so shallow. However, because we were hovering over the rods on short sessions, we were able to hit slow lifts up the needles before the reel even churned. We were fishing on closed bail arms; I was using 300's and Chris was using 301's because he's cack handed. We had loads of very confident takes and we had a lot of multiple catches.

We were on critically balanced pop ups. What we would do, the pop ups were not made any differently from the bottom baits, other than we inserted a piece of polystyrene before we boiled them. We rolled them

Back she goes...

round a square of polystyrene and then the BB shot would sink them easily. We would just trim off pieces of the shot with nail clippers until they only just sank.

We were only fishing in four feet of water, but they would take quite a long time to actually reach the bottom. They would just sit on the surface of the silt. I'm sure the carp came along and they would start putting on the brakes with their pecs and the pop ups would fluff up in front of them on a nine or ten inch hook link. This would be very provocative and I'm sure that's the reason we caught so many fish.

We had a good bait going in which they obviously wanted, and secondly, our pop up fished in the middle of quite a heavily baited area would stand out like a sore thumb because they would waft up as soon as the carp came into the swim.

I stayed at Cutt Mill right until the end of the season. In fact, I did the whole winter there and had a number of fish. Along with the fish that we had caught at Plank Island and the few I had caught at Oakmere, it ended up being a fantastic season.

Freedom again

16 — Heaven Found

After the 1984/85 season, it was all new waters again, forever on the search. One water that I had been trying to get into for many years was a little private syndicate, a tiny old gravel pit fairly close to where I live, called Fir Tree Pond.

This is quite an exceptional water; there are only a few anglers who fish it and it is kept on a very limited syndicate basis. It's been almost in a time warp. The lake has been kept very well stocked, not with numbers of fish, but quality fish. It's very unusual to catch anything under twenty pounds; in the seasons that I have fished there I have only ever caught a couple of fish under that weight. There is probably something in the region of twenty eight twenties in there, up to thirty pounds.

It is a special water, with special fish – they are all pretty fish. It is one of those waters that has been carefully and painstakingly looked after over the years. The right strains have been put in there, the right stocking levels. The swims are quite something, they actually plant vegetation in the swims! They aren't the wide, open spaces as with many venues.

It's very well looked after and it's almost like it was at Stuarts. It is a pleasant water; the fish are lovely, of course they are. It is a pleasure to be there, fishing for carp. You're on your own and it's very unusual to find yourself there with another angler, so it's you up against the carp and not the carp angler. It's almost a 'back to basics' type of water. It's a very good stalking water. The fish aren't easy to catch, they don't really come out that many times in a season. Usually, they all manage to come out at least once a season, although there are always a couple of particularly elusive ones in there, as there are in most waters. It was another piece of Heaven, somewhere to get away from it all. Whenever I felt there was any pressure on me, I would slip away to Fir Tree. Because Cutt Mill was still fishing, was a very busy water, it sometimes got a little bit too much when you had to hassle for swims. If you are being successful, you invariably get people either side of you and you end up with five yards to cast in and it can all get a bit frustrating, so when things get on top of you, it's somewhere to go and get away from it all and you can be well assured that you won't see another angler.

Therefore, it was a water that I was very glad to get into. In fact, it is one of the only waters, other than Burton, that I fished for any length of time. I will usually fish a water for a season, maybe two, at the most and go on to another water. I either get slightly fed up with a place, looking at the same scenery, or even, catching the same fish, so I generally move on. I'm not an angler who really adopts a water and stays on there for many seasons.

My old mate, Ron Buss, he's been on the Send Pit for as long as anyone can remember and he enjoys every minute of it. He's caught just about all the fish and has probably caught them many times, but it's not for me – I like to move on. There are just the couple of exceptions. One was Burton; I fell in love with the place and actually moved to live in the area to be near it, but unfortunately the fish died and really, I suppose Fir Tree has taken its place. It's one of those ponds that I think I will fish for as long as I can. It's just sheer enjoyment, completely different to Plank Island; a small water, a hard water.

At Fir Tree the carp don't suffer fools lightly. It's a creepy water and you're often crawling around on all fours. As with most waters, the margins fish extremely well, but more so here than anywhere. The margins are the features in this particular pit. Lots of overhanging trees and bushes and the carp generally spend ninety five per cent of their

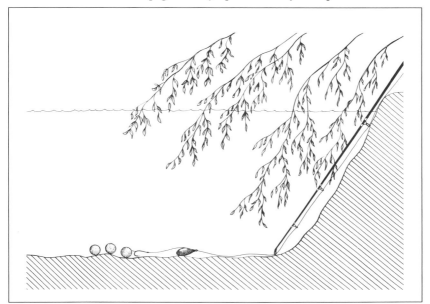

'Stalking at Fir Tree'

time within inches of the bank. To creep up on them you have got to be a fairly stealthy angler; a heavy footfall in the wrong place and the fish have gone. They've seen it all before, as they are not young fish at all. Many of them will be in excess of thirty years old and have been fished for for that length of time, so they have seen just about everything. It's not a water where heavy baiting works; it is one of those exceptions to the rule. Although I've got this thing about heavy baiting, it doesn't work at Fir Tree. Invariably, hook baits are the best tactic. A small baiting up session occasionally holds their interest for a little while, but usually not for very long. It may be days rather than weeks and by putting a lot of bait in you can decrease your chances very quickly, so it is stalking, opportunist type fishing. They won't take surface baits any more. Now that is a statement that is very difficult to make because I have never found a water anywhere where fish won't take floaters, but these fish have been caught on floaters so many times before that they just won't have it any more.

Although we're moving now into the mid eighties and slightly different materials were becoming available I was still on the Dacron type materials. The sort of thing I would be using would be camouflage Dacrons, different colour Dacrons, greens and browns rather than the bulk standard black. Colours that blended into the bottom rather more.

I had felt quite confident using tens and twelves for these very large, upper twenty carp that were in Fir Tree, on fairly heavy tackle, certainly using in excess of 10lb B.S. line for most of the time. This was snag fishing and invariably hook and hold tactics were the order of the day. I would be on 8 foot, little, short, stalking rods most of the time with the centre pin reel. Other times just with a Mitchell 300. A lot of fish were caught on the float; I did a lot of float fishing there.

I started to have success on Fir Tree Lake virtually immediately. It was right up my street because it was a stalking water and when you stalk fish, it often happens instantly. Where you can see fish in the water and you can present a bait to the fish, then you know that you've got a good chance of catching them, if you can creep up on them quietly and haven't spooked them before you put the bait in the water. I was still fishing at Cutt Mill. A bit of a revolution had taken place there. Chris and I were still fishing there and, of course, it had been a long, hot summer that year; that was undoubtedly the turning point. Although surface baits had been very successful there for a number of years, at Cutt Mill it was the year of the Chum Mixer. Chris, as many people will know, is a true advocate of surface fishing, especially with Chum Mixer. He completely capitalised on the situation. I was starting to lose interest a bit because there were very few fish that we hadn't caught there so it was seeing the same old faces again (carp, I mean), which was taking the edge off it for me. I was fishing other waters, so there was more to interest me, other than Cutt Mill, but Chris had a marvellous season that year. He had a tremendous number of fish off the surface, which was fantastic. There were many times when Chris would call me up at home and ask me to go down to photograph a twenty or a brace of twenties for him. The other anglers were very slow to catch on at first and they would still be sitting behind their rods.

Because of what had happened, they had gone off their clipped up methods and tried to copy what we had been doing; they hadn't moved on. Of course, Chris was way in front of them and he was now taking fish off the surface while all these lads were still fishing on pop ups, on slack lines, as we had been doing before. They were catching a few fish but, again, the lion's share of the fish was coming to the guy who was fishing differently.

Chris was very good at fishing the controller style and he would use a very light controller on 6lb line, size 12 or size 10 Super Specialist hooks. They are quite cute fish at the Mill; at the end of the day, they have been fished for for many years and you don't get roaring takes off the surface.

Nearly a leather

You have to get the strike timed absolutely right to ensure that you are going to make contact with a fish and he was very successful at this type of fishing. We always managed to pick out the biggest mouth out there, because that's all we could see. It was quite a coloured water; the only way you could select the larger fish was literally by the size of its mouth, which sometimes worked out and sometimes didn't. There were some long, skinny fish with big heads and big mouths in there!

What a tragedy to lose carp like this at Burton

Send Pond and a beautiful mirror

A magnificent Fir Tree mirror

An upper 20 caught whilst stalking

17 — Heaven Once More

I was still in contact with Ron Buss. We had struck up a friendship and Ron was very interested in a lake down in Hampshire, near Ringwood, called Kingfisher.

We had often spoken about this place and I was quite intrigued by it because it was another of those nice gravel pits. It operated on a ticket basis and, at that time, we could get a weekly ticket. We did four days on the first session. Ron doesn't drive and at the time I had a Mini Metro. I'll never forget it; for this relatively short trip I had loaded up the car with all my gear, enough to do the session with – and probably 100lb of bait, knowing me. I arrived at Ron's house and he looked as if he had ten times more stuff than I had!

As I said, he's a big guy and, eventually, with his knees around his neck, we made our way down to Ringwood in a very uncomfortable state, with rods sticking out of the windows and bait pile up to the gunnels. Boy, was I glad when we arrived – it was a glorious moment when we actually went through the gate and I could get out of the car and stretch my legs again!

Ron is one of my friends; I don't fish with one person, I fish with various people. Ron is a very good angler; Chris Ball is a very good angler, as is Jan Wenczka and they are my three main pals. We do have this grapevine where we are honest with each other. Although we all go off our different ways we tell each other what we are about; it's good team work as you can always capitalise on the situation. When you have got three or four people all pooling their ideas, especially if you're fishing the same water, not necessarily at the same time, it can work extremely well. This has worked out on so many occasions. Chris might ring me up and say, 'Andy, I can't get to a particular water where the fish are going'. He'll tell me where they are, in some corner or other, I'll go down there and they will be exactly where Chris has said they are and I catch them; I am able to stack them up like breeze blocks.

To get back to Kingfisher Lake. Ron had been there a couple of times and he had been reasonably successful. We arrived at Mr. Clark's house (the owner) and stood on the lawn. It was a lovely place and I had never seen swims like them in my life before. They were all mown and they had rose beds between them. The facilities were great – showers, loos and a clubhouse. It's quite an amazing place but unfortunately, it isn't open to everyone any more for it is now operated on a very exclusive ownership/membership syndicate basis. I was lucky, for I had a few sessions there before things changed. The first one was very memorable. We had done a tour of the lake; it is probably thirty-forty acres, a nice, big, open gravel pit, a few islands here and there, a couple of bays. Stacks of carp, lots of doubles, lots of twenties at the time. I think the biggest to come out from there was around 29lb. There were a lot of commons in there, as well as mirrors, which was nice because I hadn't fished that many waters with many commons in; they just weren't available. The commons that I had access to were generally singles and doubles, with very few twenties, so it was nice to have a few 20lb commons in front of us.

We walked round the lake and sighted the fish from right outside the big house, on Mr. Clark's lawn, against the long island. There were a lot of fish showing out there at very long range. It's actually been measured out to the island – it's known to be 110 yards and I wanted to put the baits up the side of it. I had the wind behind me and, at the time, I was on Tricast rods and I was using 12ft 2½lb rods with a 2½oz lead and a shock

Return to Kingfisher

leader and 8lb line. I was actually over casting, which is ironic at 110 yards. I was getting into all sorts of trouble, getting caught up in the trees.

After twenty minutes I had a 27lb mirror on the bank, which was great. It was, I think, an easy water at the time because there was no one fishing it on a regular basis. They were fairly naive fish. It was marvellous.

Anyway, out went the normal, compulsory (for me) 2,000 baits. I was fishing with three rods and into fish straight away, so it was a great start. Poor old Ron didn't fare so well on that session. He never caught a carp at all, even though he put a lot of bait out. He is a very good angler and a strong believer in this heavy baiting, but he had done something to his mix. Something was not quite right, it was a little bit on the soft side and although we fished in adjacent swims and fishing over the same very large shoal of carp, he had what we called the 'screaming greenies'. I think he ended up with about seventy tench, which was very frustrating for him because I think I had seven twenties that first session, as well as a load of doubles. I had a nice 20lb common as well, which was great, but poor old Ron just sat there, pulling in these tench, one after the other.

During that first session Mr. Clark said that the next year he was going to put it up for this multiple ownership. I then decided that I would go there as many times as I possibly could. I think I ended up fishing it seven times in all and taking quite a number of fish. I had a twenty eight pounder that very first session, which I never bettered. That was my largest fish from Kingfisher.

Things were progressing on the tackle front. The A.B.U. Cardinal 55's were the vogue reel of the time, which was quite ironic, because they weren't a carp reel at all. They were reels that had been designed with one of the first skirted spools, push button spool, very good bail alarm system on it; they just fitted quite well into carp fishing. Rods have come on in leaps and bounds and, of course, in the mid to late 1980's this compromise of a casting rod that felt nice for playing fish was starting to look good. The new carbon fibres that were coming through were a much nicer material to work with and you could have a lower diameter rod with a more progressive through type action and these would cast very well.

I was, at the time, completely sold on Tri-casts, they were nice rods and I got on with them very well. Their two piece, 12ft, 2½ and 2¼lb test curve rods were quite amazing – they really took some punishment. You could cast a tremendous distance with them. The ringing has changed, the

Fuji silicone carbide ring was all the rage. We were getting a lot of influence from the shore beach casting anglers who were using fixed spool reels. They were only using five rings and we followed the pattern, we were now down to seven rings on a 12ft rod, which was unheard of ten years before.

One of two fish at once!

18 — Chance to Reflect

I have not usually stayed on one lake; I have only fished most lakes for one year or, at most, two years but I keep returning to Fir Tree Lake. Well it is almost my little bit of Redmire. I think we are always searching for these fairly exclusive waters where we feel at home. Certainly Fir Tree Lake is that for me. I like the small band of anglers who fish there and I try not to hammer it. I'm sure if I concentrated on it for a complete season I could catch all the fish probably two or three times. Rather than do that, I want it to last for many years. I don't really consider not joining it again. It's that little bit of heaven that I think we are all searching for and I can feel almost at peace with the world when I go there, with no pressure on me at all. Sometimes I catch fish and sometimes I don't, but I really enjoy the atmosphere there.

It's a very prolific twenties water for medium size to big twenties. It has produced fish up to 37lb in the past and I believe it will again. Some of the fish that are there now have been thirties in the past.

I started writing on a fairly regular basis in the early years of the C.A.A. I was then invited to write for various monthly magazines and also the weeklies. This was on a regular basis as it was a series; each article would be on a particular theme – on floater fishing, winter carp fishing or baits, or whatever. This writing seemed to escalate over the years. I never ever set out, in any period of my life, to become an angling writer. I started writing about my experiences and people found it interesting and it has gone on from there. You do have your own style and it puts a stamp on your writing. Rod Hutchinson is the same. I haven't been influenced by anyone else. I enjoy other people's pen work, certainly Rod's and Harry Haskell's. I really do enjoy their writing.

All I do is try to put down on paper my own thoughts and there is very little speculation in what I write. It's actually based around personal experences. I hope it is that which has kept everything on a sensible level and not escalated out of all recognition.

I did some 'Carry on Carping' articles for the Angler's Mail and more recently I have been writing a regular column for the paper; I'm now in my sixth year, which is the longest running specialist carp column on a weekly basis which has been known, so that is very nice. In fact, it is very difficult to project it too much above the fundamental level at which I write. Most readers, judging by the vast amount of mail I receive, ask very fundamental questions. Most people really don't want to know what the latest bait is, or about the latest rig. They haven't had that much experience as regards finding a particular water with carp in, or even how to approach that water, let alone the latest all singing set ups.

I got tied up writing for the weekly and monthly magazines and the one thing that I actually did want to do was to write a book. I did feel there was a need for a basic book on carp fishing to be written. There are a lot of very good books about; 'Quest for Carp' has certainly got to be my all time favourite. I still read it now and it does capture a lot of the romantic magic and mystery about carp fishing. Also, there is 'Carp Fever', which is the best selling carp book to date and I doubt if it will ever be surpassed in terms of sales. The book I wanted to write was a completely different book and was eventually published by Hamlyn as Andy Little's Big Carp Book.

One of the waters featured in the book was Willow Park. It's a very prolific water, full of singles and doubles. There must be hundreds of them in there and they are very pretty fish. It is a water that really hasn't been hammered by the carp angler and the restrictions are such on there

'Over the moon' with this fish

that I don't think it ever will be. It is a pleasurable water – which are few and far between these days – where you can go for a day's fishing and have the chance of catching a fair number of carp; a dozen carp in a day at Willow Park is not at all unusual.

The very first time I went down there, I had a quick recce round and cast a lead around to see what the bottom was like. It is a fairly even one and although there are a few bars, there's four to five feet of water over most of them. The far end, where the two bays branch out in either direction, is deeper water and it is more silty there, but because there are other water sports on there, mainly wind surfing, the carp are always kept on the move. There are so many carp in the water that you could really settle in a number of positions and be in with a good chance of having multiple catches of decent sized fish.

I've got some lovely memories of Willow Park. It is tremendous. I've had some good catches there and it has always been a water I have got a soft spot for. It is a pretty water, considering the area. It is in a very heavily populated part of the Surrey/Hampshire border, which is situated adjacent to a housing estate.

As the name implies, there are lots of willow trees round it. Unfortunately, it has been subject to development work and is currently

Willow Park linear upper double

undergoing some restoration work. Sadly, some banks have eroded and some of the willow trees have had to be removed, but it still has the nice scenery and a lot of its character has been kept. It is not heavily fished and you don't have to compete with loads of carp anglers. It is good for taking friends and colleagues to fish with you. Also, it's a nice spot for photographic work. They are such lovely looking fish; there's a balance probably of something like fifty/fifty commons and mirrors in there. Very pretty fish, lots of linear, some fully scaled, even a few twenty pounders, so there are a lot to fish for.

My first book was a basic instruction book on carp fishing. The whole idea was that we wouldn't rely on tired old information. I really wanted to catch carp from all parts of the country, not just go to my local water where I knew I could catch twenties and maybe thirties, but to find new waters where I have never fished before. In the course of preparing the book I certainly went to at least six different counties to fish new waters that I had never seen before and caught carp from them all and, I'm glad to say, on all sorts of varying tactics. I caught a beautiful 20lb two tone common from a difficult water in Hampshire. This was on a floater.

We went to some quite hard syndicate waters at Birmingham, using a completely different method, very long range fishing, over one hundred yards in quite adverse conditions and, again, managed to put a very nice twenty pounder on the bank – a mirror this time. So, for that year, I did sacrifice settling on any one particular water. There was no baiting programme at all for that year. I didn't know where I was going to be fishing from one week to the next and we obviously relied on the weather for photography. It took eighteen months to complete the book.

One of the waters I wrote about in the book was a water known as Sway Lake. This was right at the other end of the scale, a very commercial water. It started life as a trout fishery, situated down at Lyndhurst in Hampshire. The guy who owned these lakes, Tim Clarke, is the brother of Chris Clarke, the successful sea angler. Tim lives on the site and he originally dug them out as a trout fishery but he decided to turn one of them over to a coarse/carp fishery. This is a completely different water; a very thin, long narrow section of water, quite heavily stocked with very pretty fish, but it was really heavily fished. I was quite amazed; people were about every ten yards along the bank, and closer in some areas. I was staggered by the number of anglers who were there and it was hard to really get anything going at all.

If you can imagine, something less than twenty five yards wide, for the most part, with people down both banks... It has to be said, it's a pretty little place, with some lovely looking fish in there, but not a water that I would personally choose to go and fish if I had the choice.

On the days that we did fish there, I caught more than anyone else, but I think really, the calibre of the anglers who were fishing there had a lot to do with it. There were lots of beginners, as it is a day ticket water. If you have a little bit on the special side, baiting up, or rigs you can easily catch with... You had to be fairly accurate to make sure that you gave yourself the best chance. It wasn't mass baiting there at all; very small pockets of bait, then just dropping either a float fished boilie or a semi bolt rig type set up, into these little patches. Quite weedy water, with a few snags here and there, so there were little, clear areas where the fish had been feeding – they had cleared them by their intense movements. I think it was finding these little spots that helped me sort a few fish out. It wasn't by doing anything clever, it was just a little bit of common sense, nothing else.

Another water mentioned in the book is one called Old Bury Hill, which is known mainly for its zander potential – there is a terrific head of zander.Quite a unique water – one of the only still waters in that part of the world where you have got zander and probably almost to record size. They have been caught there in excess of 14lb, some real monsters. This is another commercial fishery; it used to be owned by Graham Rowles. Completely different from Sway Lakes as it is a much larger lake. Also it only had the minimal opportunity for stalking; most of the fish we caught there were from sitting behind the rods.

When we were picking these waters, we tried to come up with what the other anglers were going to find problematic and the tench, now that they have switched on to boilies, certainly at Bury Hill, are indeed that.

I tried to get over this problem by selecting the carp against these large numbers of tench. I wasn't allowed to use any hard baits there, such as hazelnuts, Brazil nuts or tiger nuts, so it was really down to the boilies and trying to find a technique or a bait that would be more selective to give me a better chance of catching the carp.

It was virtually an impossible task to completely eliminate tench. I was reasonably successful, as I could get the carp to a stage of preoccupation with the boilies and they would push the tench out of the swim, but naturally, you had to catch quite a few tench before that situation actually arose. The idea was, that I would get myself into an area of the lake where I knew there was going to be large amounts of carp moving through, and it was almost a baiting syndrome once again. I put a lot of bait in this area. These spots were under bushes against the far island, and only about four feet square, so I had to be accurate with my casting at reasonable range. Sixty yards would put me against an island, and baiting up very tight under those bushes where I knew the carp were moving along, had to be spot on. This meant I was getting a concentration of carp feeding which eventually moved the tench out. I might catch four or five tench first but as soon as the first carp was hooked I knew that there was probably twenty, or maybe thirty fish in the swim and very often I would catch a dozen of those fish in a very short time before they moved off.

I had mirrors up to mid twenties; also a couple of low 20lb commons as well, which was lovely. There was a real hotch potch of strains in there. Because Graham Rowles was in the fishery management business, he had access to fish from literally all over the country so he was sometimes left with some carp on his hands and they went into Old Bury Hill.

There are some nice photographs in the book too. Talking of photographs, it's all changed hasn't it? When I started carp fishing I didn't even own a camera and photographs were not that important. Eventually, I did get a little Instamatic job and took some snapshots.

I look back at some of the old photographs from the fifties and sixties and cringe at the quality of them. I think it's a sign of the times that now, with the glossy magazines and the very good reproductions we can see around us, with the numerous carp specialist magazines, it has come on in leaps and bounds. Likewise with the videos; I never thought they would take off.

When Clive and Malcolm first did their videos, I thought that would be it, the end of it, but there are dozens of them now. There are lots of people like Mick Hall who have done very good amateur videos. They are not in the same league as the likes of Hugh Miles, but certainly they are very entertaining. I'm looking forward to seeing the 'Carp in Winter' videos because I was one of the anglers who suffered in the course of making those films.

One point here, there is no justification at all in keeping a fish out of the water any longer than is necessary. The welfare of the carp will not, and should not, suffer for a video, or any other reason.

After the videos, television. We've seen what John Wilson has done. It has really taken off well. He has probably done more for the image of angling than anyone in its history.

I have been fairly lightly involved on London Weekend Television. I was invited to appear on the 6 O'Clock Show with Michael Aspel and Danny Baker. The filming took all day for a four or five minute slot on the programme. Danny Baker, a complete non-angler and a very nice guy, was accompanied by his make up lady and the production team of about half a dozen people!

I was actually approached direct by London Weekend Television to do the fishing on my own at first. I refused, saying under no circumstances did I feel qualified to do this on my own. It was major television for angling, as this was prior to the John Wilson days.

The approach line was quite fantastic – 'Hello, Mr. Little. You are a good, well known carp angler. Please can we come for a day's filming with you and can you come on Friday (or whatever day it was) and catch a forty pounder from Yateley?'

I replied, 'Well, what time would you like me to catch this forty pounder, seeing as I have never caught one before, we might as well put a time limit on it!'

It was difficult to explain to these non-anglers that I could not just go out and catch a forty pound carp to order. I said it was virtually impossible to do so. I suggested it might be a good idea to invite other carp anglers along who had caught forty pound carp and I could think of three who would probably like to come along – Chris Yates, Robin Dix and Ritchie McDonald. They all agreed and Peter Mohan came along as well. He was responsible for starting the British Carp Study group and later, the Carp Anglers' Association, which were the first specialist carp groups.

Some time during the afternoon, while they were filming – there were lots of retakes – when suddenly there was a shout from the corner of the Car Park Lake. A young lad by the name of Terry had actually hooked one of the biggest fish in the complex, 'Heather the Leather', which was the one that Robin Dix had caught at forty pounds plus the previous season. They managed to film this for the show but it missed the mark by a few ounces – so they very nearly had their forty pounder on TV, which was quite something for us lads. Having said that it was impossible, Terry almost pulled it off, so that was great. It made us all look very silly, having told this television crew that here were the best carp anglers in the world and they said it was almost impossible to predict being able to catch a forty pounder, especially from somewhere like Yateley!

So now we were back to winter again and I decided against fishing Cutt Mill. By now I had caught all the carp I wanted from there. I did not fancy catching the same old fish again. There was the same pressure for new waters so I was lucky to get into another water in the area, another quite famous carp water near Haslemere, called Badger Pool. This very famous water has been fished by some very good anglers like Dennis Smale and Chris Yates, to name just a couple. It was nice because it had quite a few 20lb commons in it. It's a very weedy water, lots of lily pads and Canadian pond weed in there, almost floor to ceiling for most of the time. The first year, I didn't fish it much, as I joined during the summer months when writing my first book, but I managed to get some time there during the winter. The weed had died down quite a bit and there were fewer anglers about. This nice thing was, it was completely different again from anything that I had fished before. It had massive fir trees all the way round it.

There was one private bank where you couldn't fish and, for me, the method was to fish tight under this private bank in the far margins and you would catch the carp patrolling up and down this area.

The biggest problem that I encountered was that you had to get your bait underneath the branches. Also they had to land in a very tight area to get takes, but I had a problem because I didn't want to use short hook links there. With the silt and the decaying weed, and everything else, I felt it would be better to use long hook links but it was very difficult to cast a three foot hook link underneath those branches. I had to rig up some weird and wonderful set ups that I could actually do this with. In the end I used a running rig, which consisted of two Drennan rings which were pulled back and PVA'd together. I also PVA'd a small

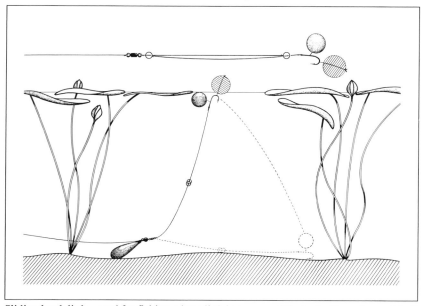

Sliding hook link – used for fishing a long link in very small holes in lily pads – polyball and shortened hook link are PVA'd

polyball on the bend of the hook so I was able to cast out an eighteen inch trace quite well into those gaps underneath the bushes. Invariably I would put one wrap of PVA round the main hook link and two or three wraps around the polyball on the bend of the hook. The hook link one would dissolve first and then would gradually expand the hook link out to its full length of three feet and would then come to the surface. That way I could be sure everything was tangle free and the whole rig would have a very soft landing on top of the weed. It was an amazingly successful set up and quite a few other people at Badger Pool adopted it because it wasn't something that I particularly wanted to keep quiet. We caught a lot of fish that winter.

I caught two twenty pound commons as well as two or three twenty pound mirrors, so it was a nice end to the season for me. It was a season which had really been one of dashing up and down the country, not being able to settle on one particular water, but for the last few weeks of the season I was able to do my own thing for a change, which was great.

19 — Final Frontier

Slide shows were fairly new. Usually at the NASA conferences, the CAA conferences and those sort of events you would just get up and talk – there were no slides to accompany the talk. In fact, we didn't have that much photographic material to back it up. I honestly don't know when I did my first slide show, it was probably some time in the seventies. I was certainly doing them at local meetings before Savay. In the early days you didn't have crowds in the numbers that we have at the conferences now. It was a small gathering of mates and invariably it all started at local club level, or at a local CAA meeting, where the total audience was no more than fifty people.

Needless to say, getting up in front of fifty people is nowhere near as daunting as standing on the stage at Wembley with a thousand faces looking at you. We are not professionals and I'm sure people take that into consideration. I understand how people must feel, standing up for the first time in front of a huge audience – some of the lads currently doing it must be shaking in their boots, they really must, so full credit to them for having a go.

It's always nice to start with a fish at the beginning of a season. I'm glad to say that we haven't yet abolished the close season. I like there to be beginnings and endings. I look forward to March 14th when we hang our rods up for a few months. I then look ahead to June 16th with great expectations.

I always like June 16th to be a little bit special. I haven't missed many June 16ths over the years I have been carp fishing and with most of them I have always tried to create something that I haven't done before, like Savay – that was a magnificent start to the season; Oakmere was the same.

1986-87, I'd finished the year at the Badger Pool. The next season I decided I'd go to Fir Tree. The main reason was that I was going to be virtually on my own. It wasn't like the Darenth years. June 16th at Darenth was quite an unbelievable event. What would actually happen was that we would arrive at the car park and we would have a rod rest in our hands and that would be it. They blew a whistle and off you ran to claim your spot and put your rod rest in. Thankfully, all that has changed. I'm too old for that game these days and to start off at Fir Tree with a leisurely start was just right.

I got up early in the morning and went down there, did the first day and I think I did the night as well. I had a couple of nice fish – I think I had a 27lb leather and a 24lb mirror. It was a nice, leisurely start to the season with no one else about. Very pleasant fishing.

There were a number of waters that I was fishing at that time. I certainly wanted to look at the Thames again, it was a water that I particularly wanted to fish. The Thames has always held a great fascination for me and it was somewhere that I really wanted to have a proper crack at – I have always dabbled at it. It's certainly one of the last frontiers to be explored but there are lots of problems on the Thames. It's not an easy water to approach. For a start, it's far bigger than anything else, it is one of the biggest carp waters in the country. The carp are very nomadic, you can be on a fish one day and that same fish can be five miles away the next day. They don't respond to boilies very readily in the Thames. They do so on other major rivers but the Thames is hard going on boilies. The carp are really eating baits that lots of other fish will be feeding on so you've got to make sure that you have got your areas just right, otherwise you are going to do a lot of fishing and not catch many carp.

Location is paramount, as with any water, and even more so in the Thames than anywhere else, that's for sure. The biggest problem with the Thames is the heavy boat traffic, especially during the daylight hours. It's also difficult at night in the summer, with the disco boats etc., travelling on the river. The carp very rarely show themselves during the daytime. I have found that the best time to spot carp in the Thames is actually after midnight and before first light in the morning, so to try to locate fish I would walk the tow paths during those hours.

I would pick an area that I fancied, or had known carp to come out of in matches, or the odd one that had fallen to a barbel angler or whatever, and I would just walk the tow paths in the small hours of the morning. Invariably, after a few early mornings of doing this, some sort of pattern would emerge, when carp would show themselves in a similar spot at the same sort of time.

I spent so much time putting boilies in and it was a waste – it just didn't work. By far the best bait for the Thames is probably maggots. They are not selective enough, that is the problem. Luncheon meat failed miserably too. I caught loads of chub on it; it also caught bream and barbel, but very few carp.

Hemp certainly attracted them in, but again we had lots of problems with roach and dace and everything else. Sweetcorn was the only selective bait that I found was a constant winner and was acceptable to the Thames carp. On this bait we caught the odd few bream and chub, but it was the carp which took an instant liking to the corn. It was big beds of bait again – I keep on about the baiting syndrome, but it's so very important. Once you have located your fish, you have got to do something to turn the tables in your favour. Initially, I would put hemp down and it would attract everything into the swim. I'm sure the attentions of the roach and dace etc., in turn, drew the carp into the swim. Over the top of the hemp we would put pounds and pounds of sweetcorn. That's the way things went. I only very rarely caught carp in the daytime and if I did, it would be just at daybreak. By far, most were caught during the hours of darkness.

There are some absolute monsters in the Thames. As time passed I managed to get a couple of thirties out of it. In most recent years, my personal best English common of 33lb came from there and that was really fantastic. There are, undoubtedly, 40lb carp in the Thames and they are there to be caught.

At first I thought I had found another little piece of heaven that no one else should ever hear about. As it is such a big river, I was slightly dubious at first of even mentioning it. I have since written articles about

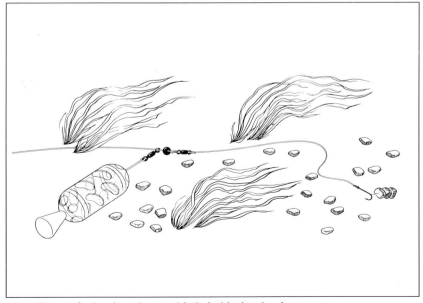

River Thames feeder rig – elongated hole in blockend to let out corn

A mid-20 fully scaled carp

One of seven 20's

Back to Fir Tree and success once again

Andy's son with a lovely 20.8 common

it and showed quite a lot of slides about my exploits on the Thames. There are still very few people who fish the Thames for carp because of all the problems I have previously mentioned. Certainly, my friends' approach to carp angling has made our slide shows slightly different to other people's. I say 'our' slide shows because I have been teamed up with Chris Ball now for several years and we have this little rapport between us. What we tend to do, rather than show various slides of one fish and it going back to the water and swimming away, we have very few slides but every slide tells a story; because they do, nearly every capture of carp has a story; or sometimes it's just a water that we show and explain why we failed on it for one reason or another, but there's always a story. I think it's good for the youngsters coming into the sport to see more than just picture after picture of big carp.

We do catch little carp and in our slide shows we include the small fish because each, in their own way, has meant something. Whether it's a five pounder or, hopefully, one of these days, a fifty pounder, they all mean something to us in varying degrees. It's more than likely there have been problems that we have encountered on the way before the fish finally came to the bank.

20 — Patshull

Over the years I have caught various carp, linears, mirrors, leathers and commons. However, I have got a preference for commons and the reason I'm so fond of them is because I have caught so few of them. I've never had as many big commons in front of me during my angling career as at the Church Pool at Patshull; even at Savay, although there are only one or two very large, famous commons in there.

At Send there were only one or two 20lb commons. I have never been on a water where there are predominantly commons above mirrors. There are quite a few of them about, but generally in the Surrey and Hampshire area, and even in Kent, it was unheard of in my early fishing days. There were very few commons. My first 20lb common was actually not until 1980 when I fished Savay. I had never caught a 20lb common until then. Loads of 20lb mirrors, but no 20lb commons so my great interest in commons, in fishing for them, is because I haven't caught that many of them.

Certainly the Patshull Shropshire syndicate water that is so well publicised these days, was one that I had my eye on for quite a while. When it changed over from day ticket to being a syndicate, I tried to get in there but the membership was fairly limited. It wasn't until a couple of years later that I managed to secure a place on the syndicate. It is the complete opposite for some of the lads who regularly fish it, all they want to do is to catch the very light stock of mirrors that are in there. There is one famous 30lb mirror in there that everyone wants to catch but that is the last big fish that I want to catch there! I can honestly say, I struggled on this water. It has a large head of twenty pound commons in there, going right up to 30lb but I found it a very difficult water. The main problem was that I was usually fishing it just at weekends and it is a busy water. There were always a lot of people about and there were loads of eels present and I couldn't do my own thing.

The eels were a real problem. I wanted to put a load of bait in and the eels restricted my movements. I would bait up with several thousand boilies and the eels would come into the swim and completely clear them off before the carp even got a look in. Despite their interference, I did manage to catch the odd carp there. I had a few 20lb commons, but I would consider it one of the waters that I have actually failed on.

The problem was that it wasn't a local water where I could be first down; my edge had been destroyed, but you make the sacrifice in order to catch something you want. A 20lb common means more to me than a 30lb mirror; I have caught so few of them.

There are some very proficient anglers on there who catch fish very regularly and they catch lots of them. I'm definitely not in that category. I struggled at Patshull. I was arriving there after a two hundred mile drive, feeling very tired and not wanting to have a good look round. As there were very few swims left, I would have to drop into one of them and

Patshull mirror

try to make the best of what was in front of me. I had no edge at all, there was nothing I could do to create that very important edge, so I was really up against it. It would usually be that the fish that came my way were taken off the surface, or were caught with tiger nuts fished over a small bed of hemp and really there were no situations that I could capitalise on. I think if I did live nearby I could get the baiting act together; I would overcome the eel problems and the competition for swims.

Having said that, I knew what I was letting myself in for when I fished up there. I knew it was going to be hard going, but nevertheless, I enjoyed the time I was there. I shall probably fish it for several more seasons and hopefully catch the odd twenty pound common as the situation arises.

The only time I thought I was anywhere near getting my act together was on a few slightly longer winter sessions. Right throughout the winter, the weekends still appeared to be very busy but I did manage to sneak off and get a couple of midweek sessions in. In fact, on one of them, for the first time ever, I was confronted with the whole lake to myself for three complete days. During those three days I moved swims six or seven times until I eventually found some feeding carp and caught a brace of twenties during the course of one night and had a further take on which the hook pulled after ten minutes. Isn't it ironic, on a water that is usually so busy, when you need someone to take some photos there is no one there. However, a passing dog walker kindly obliged and although the results were nothing spectacular, at least I have a record of the catch.

The other winter session where it all started to come right, but eventually ended in disaster, was when I found some fish feeding tight under the dam wall against some extending tree roots. I managed two takes in six hours, both of which broke me on some unseen underwater snag.

The lads there were very helpful and guys like Rob Hale, John Freeman and Sean Harrison could not have been more informative and it was a pleasure fishing with them. I was most impressed with the ability of all three, but more so with John Freeman. He was at one with the water and I would think ninety per cent of the fish he caught at Patshull were by stalking. He would creep around in the reed beds and margins in chest waders, stalking his fish like a heron and with such intimate knowledge of the water, he seemed to have the ability of knowing where the carp were going to be even before they did themselves.

When he couldn't stalk them, he would ambush them. John, not being one for convention, would set his rods up in the middle of the reed beds and fish his bait in tiny, tight areas that he knew the fish would eventually visit. Suddenly, there would be a burst of life from an Optonic from the centre of a reed bed. You would then see John hurriedly donning his waders, grabbing his net and off in pursuit of the unseen fish. I am amazed that he could find his rods half the time, especially in the middle of the night, but there can be no argument – although his tactics may be unconventional – he is the most successful angler at Patshull and at long last, after many years of trying, he has achieved his ambition of catching a thirty pound common from the water.

I am grateful for the hours I spent chatting with John, one of the top stalking anglers in the country.

I had good results on the famous Dog Island Lake. A peculiar place, a very large, old, gravel pit somewhere round about eighty acres.

I really was taken in by this water. I had been caught out on Mike Oyez' water, and now this place. It was only because someone said there was a thirty pound common in there that I fished it, although as there was also supposed to be a forty pound mirror in there I didn't need much persuading to fish there, as you can imagine. There was very limited night fishing there, you had to get a special licence. To be fair, it wasn't too much of a problem getting into the club, but obtaining night tickets was a problem. However, I did manage to get one the first season I fished there.

As I said, it was quite a big water, about eighty acres. There are a lot of islands, a lot of places for the carp to get away and there are lots of carp in there. I did manage to catch stacks of doubles and a few twenties but not the monsters that were supposed to be in there.

I spent a lot of time there when really, I should have been on other waters, but I gave it my best shot. The hot spot was against a large island. After dark I would take my many bags of boilies and swim out to the large island; my mate on the main bank would direct me to the right area and we would fill the whole of the margins in with substantial amounts of bait. However, one night, whilst I was doing this, the bailiff sent his Alsatian dog after me and he managed to get on the island – but I vacated it very quickly! It was the first thirteen second, one hundred metre swim that you had ever seen in your life – I got off that island fairly rapidly! The dog wouldn't come off the island and it was there for days, just barking and barking – hence the name Dog Island.

We had lots of fish there and caught them right up to 28lb. The pair of us caught something like twenty odd twenty pounders out of there and stacks of doubles, quite a few singles but never once, even in the very hot weather, when lots of fish were on the surface, did we ever clap eyes on this thirty pound common, or this forty pound mirror.

It was very much long range tactics at Dog Island Lake. The hot spot tight against the island was in one place, probably some 120 yards cast. Here I gunned up with some 2½lb, 12ft Tri-Casts and my Mitchell 300S's. The spools were overfilled with 8lb Sylcast Mainline and a 15lb shockleader. Leads would either be 2½ or 3oz to achieve the distance. There was quite a lot of blanket weed as well as Canadian Pond Weed and to overcome any problems of the baits being buried from sight, I would usually fish a pop up directly off the lead on a 9 or 10 inch hook link or, alternatively, a critically balanced slow sinking boilie.

I had, by now, changed to soft hook links and was using Bifa braided Terylene which I found far superior to any other Dacron type materials that I had used in the past.

I was still experiencing great success with the chemically sharpened hooks and although I remember that, at the time, there was a question mark over the use of them and quite a lot of anglers were airing the view that they were damaging fish, I can honestly say that I never experienced any problems of that sort at all. I just felt that they were far superior in not only hooking ability, but in strength, than anything else that was available on the market at that time. In fact, it was the Drennan Super

An immaculate Patshull common

Specialist that I had now turned to and these were actually manufactured on slightly thicker wire than their standard counterparts, thus creating a very tough, heavily forged pattern of hook with an ultra sharp point, which was ideally suited for hair rig boilie fishing.

The boilies themselves, I had gone back to using liquidised squid and this had been such an instant bait on so many waters that I felt it was ideally suited for Dog Island. I felt with hindsight, that I had been chasing shadows as I am strongly of the opinion that those giant carp were not there during the time I fished, I had enjoyed myself.

I knew I would never return to Dog Island but it was another chapter in my carp fishing life.

21 — Carp Catcher Antics

The one lake where I got more successful as time went on was the Broad-water Lake where the Charity Carp Catch is held. Broadwater is the opposite end of the scale to what most people specialise in carp for. This is such an overstocked water, it is quite remarkable.

It is a public park and a club water. It's a smashing little place where you can go down for the day, especially if you have been struggling on some other water, and be assured of catching carp. I love it there, I really do. It's a place where I can take the kids and they can catch them too.

They have the Charity Carp Catch every year; they support good causes and various charities such as leukemia and cancer research. It's not meant to be a match or any sort of competition, it's meant to raise money, but inevitably, when you get a bunch of anglers together there is bound to be some competition. They say we don't match fish but I think we are the biggest load of competitors ever; it's on a national scale rather than all sitting on one water. People like Chris Yates and Terry Eustace have fished there over the years and I was invited to go and fish it.

Ron Buss had fished the Charity Carp Catch the year before and he said it would be a good idea if I went down; it is by invitation only and I fished it with him. It is a cracking water because there are so many carp in there and this makes the twenty four hour Carp Catch a bit of an endurance test, because it is not lying on bedchairs, waiting for a take every couple or three hours – you are getting one or two takes every five minutes when it's really going and sometimes, two takes at the same time.

I have now fished the Godalming Charity Carp Catch for the last five years and I've somehow or other managed to get myself in the frame every year. I have won it three times and come second twice.

That very first year when I fished it with Ron Buss, there was really a lot of competition. We fished adjacent swims and from the off it was obvious that we were going to leave everyone standing. Eventually, it ended almost on the whistle that there were only ounces between us. We both caught in excess of 400lb of carp in that twenty four hours. I ended up with 439lb 7oz of carp and Ron had about 445lb in the twenty four hours, so there was very little in it. It was a bit of friendly competition so that at the end of the day we raised a lot of money. I enjoyed it as it was so different; it really is a bit of fun. The next year, the competition was even greater and even people like Ritchie MacDonald now joined in. I somehow thought it was getting out of hand and the true meaning of the event was being lost, which was a little sad, but naturally we are competitive beings and everyone is going to extract as much as they possibly can from the swim that they are fishing.

I would tend to fish it almost semi match style, even though we were sitting behind pairs of carp rods. I would bait up several parts of the swim so as one died I would move on to the next and keep alternating right throughout the twenty four hours. Although it has been said many times that it's the guy with the most boilies who is going to win, I strongly oppose that, as this particular year there was a limit of five thousand boilies, or the equivalent weight in other baits. I only used about half that amount and there were whispers running round during the event that several lads had already come near to using up their five thousand boilies within the first twelve hours of the Carp Catch. It was really a matter of keeping the baiting levels just right so that the carp were interested enough to stay in the swim and not get filled up with too many

Charity Carp Catch Match

baits, but constantly be on the lookout for more freebies to eat, therefore ensuring continuous action.

The margins would often be ignored, especially by the specialist carp anglers but I would think that over a quarter of the catches that I'd had throughout the years I had been fishing the Carp Catch had come out of the margins themselves. A handful of bait would go out under the rod tip every hour or so. You could catch a fish in the margins and then the rest would vanish, only to return only half an hour or so later. So it was back out, fishing at twenty five to fifty yards until there was evidence of carp back in the margins, thus keeping the whole thing ticking over on the three lines of attack all the time.

That second year, I actually managed to topple Terry Eustace's record with a catch of 509lb 14oz, which is still the current record for the lake. I believe that weight was made up of in excess of ninety carp and I used no more than about 2,500 boilies, proving that it's not just a matter of chucking vast amounts of bait in.

One guy I had a great deal of pleasure in watching whilst I have been attending these charity matches, is local angler David Dean. He is really into the margin fishing in a big way and attracts the carp into the swim with large beds of hemp and then fishes mini boilies over the top. His

A nice Broadwater carp is returned

tackle is quite light, only using three or four pound line to extract the fish from the swim. His skills are such that he actually gets the carp completely preoccupied on his bed of hemp, so much so that the swim resembles half a ton of fizzing Alka Seltzers. It's quite magic to watch. Continuous line bites give an indication of how many carp are present in the swim and Dave will set his rods up quite high with long drops and Fairy Liquid bottle tops, ignoring everything until the reels start to churn. It is definitely an all or nothing method of fishing and it will often take the first twelve hours of the event to build the swim up and then it becomes a real race for home. I'm sure if it was just taken on the second twelve hours total weight, Dave would win it every time. The last few hours of the match can be quite extraordinary as he is catching a fish every couple of minutes.

Naturally, with so many carp being caught, the organisers are very much reliant on the services of voluntary stewards, as each fish is weighed and documented as it is caught and immediately returned. I'm afraid the hard working stewards are somewhat the unsung heroes of the event. The Charity Carp Catch would not be the same without Alf's early morning breakfast, synonymous as the event itself. He somehow or other manages to cook and supply a full English breakfast piping hot in every competitor's swim. I could certainly do with him as a permanent gillie.

It's little touches like this that make the whole thing so pleasurable to attend.

There are usually between thirty and forty anglers who fish there. David Woods, the organiser, works extremely hard to arrange everything and he has this horrendous task of getting all these people together, making sure the money is collected in and arranging everything else. It is nice because it is the side of angling that really, I think we should promote more as the years go on, because is shows us in a very good light to the general public.

With this sport that we all enjoy so much and the vast amount of hours we put in, it is nice to be able to put something back into it so that other people, less fortunate than ourselves, can gain from it. Long may it continue and may there be many more of them.

22 — French Flirtation

It wasn't my original intention to go abroad at all. Before my first foreign trip I was firmly convinced there was so much to do in the U.K. that I had no need to go abroad to catch carp. There are many waters that I haven't fished and there are so many fish that I haven't caught, so why did I want to go abroad?

It was really my two old buddies, Chris Ball and Jan Wenczka who pulled a bit of a fast one on me. A couple of their mates had been out to the River Lot at St. Geniez down in the south of France – in the mid Pyrenees area – and they had caught some very big commons. As you have probably gathered, my passion for catching large commons is fairly well known, but what I hadn't realised up until that time was that neither Jan nor Chris had ever caught a 20lb common from anywhere in the world, let alone England. Anyway these guys had been out there and not only had they caught 20lb commons, they had caught 30lb commons, and they were Redmire lookalikes.

During the close season, they suggested that we have a little get-together and have a chat about how we mucked it all up during the previous season and how we were going to slay them all in the next season. It was during one of these get-togethers that Chris very calmly and collectively spread a load of photographs in front of me and about forty five seconds later was making plans for us to go to the south of France.

The only problem was that we had to take our wives as well – which was a story in itself. After all, it was the south of France and the local vino... Naturally, there would be no roughing it, so a hotel near to the River Lot in the town of St. Geniez was booked.

We ended up with so much stuff we decided to go in three separate cars. A forest of rods, a ton of bait and a bag full of film meant there was very little room left for the girls' sun tan lotion, as the convoy set off.

We got to Portsmouth without a hitch and arrived safe and sound at Caen after a sleepless night's crossing. With our route across France mapped out, we started to make our way south, each taking it in turns to lead. The journey was fairly uneventful until we entered the busy town of Tours where, somehow or other, we all got split up. There was much fumbling for maps and swearing by the wives, who were navigating, as we each took a different route around the town. At one stage, we all ended up at the same set of traffic lights – each going in a different direction! That was the last I saw of our companions for the next ten hours or so.

Amazingly, with the wives directing, we found ourselves negotiating the treacherous bends up through the Pyrenees. By now all the sicky bags were filled from our two young sons, who were squashed between the delightful smells of Black Cherry and Peanut Pro boilies; that, together with the incredible distance and the soaring heat had almost put paid to the holiday before it had started.

Totally convinced that both Chris and Jan were already sampling the delights of the French wine, I was surprised when we eventually drove into the forecourt and did not find their cars parked there. Somehow or other we had won the 'Gumball' rally and it was about four hours later that the rest of the gang turned up.

We got down to the business of planning our first recce for the following morning. It was agreed that we wouldn't actually fish, but just go and have a look after a leisurely breakfast.

The River Lot is dammed just above the town of St. Com-d'Olt, which changes the river completely. Below the valley it is normally flooded like a vast lake and it was around the area of Cabanac that we had our first look. We were told to expect depths in excess of 80ft in this area as the river was running fairly full, so you can imagine our surprise when we were confronted by a tiny little brook running through a vast area of mud flats. Surely this couldn't be the place? Enquiries were made and, yes, we had arrived. All those hundreds of miles and we were staring at an empty river and no carp. Surely this had to be a nightmare?

After a bit of bargaining with a local, we managed to secure the use of his boat for about 40 francs. Leaving the girls to soak up the sun, the three of us paddled down the river in search of the disappearing carp. The river looked awful, a really dirty brown colour and there was nothing that really took our fancy, but we knew we were in the right area so we planned our first assault for that afternoon.

Nothing was forthcoming, although we did see a carp or two – and it was the same story for the next four days. We tried various areas and with the exception of one carp coming adrift to my rods, it was fruitless.

The lads were really dejected by now and decided to give up on the fishing to concentrate on the food and drink and I must admit I was feeling much the same way myself. As if this wasn't bad enough, the weather had taken a turn for the worse and it had suddenly got much colder, so even the wives were moaning as they were confined to the cars during the fishing trips.

On the last but one day the river started to rise a little and as I pushed the boat out (for what I thought was the last time) that evening, the situation completely changed. The wife and boys were stuck back at the hotel; Chris and Jan, and their wives, had gone to find a cafe at one of the nearby villages, so I was on my own. As I paddled across the now rising river I was suddenly confronted by carp everywhere.

As the river began rising, the carp moved onto the mud flats and were now cavorting in eighteen inches to two feet of water. So intense was their activity that some of them actually hit the boat as I rowed out. Panic stricken, I rowed like a maniac back to the car to muster as much bait as I could carry – I definitely wasn't going to lose them now.

I scattered twenty or thirty pounds of boilies across an area of about fifty yards long by about ten yards wide where the activity was most intense. It was pitch black by now and I just had to go and tell the lads. I drove from village to village until I finally found their cars. I ran into the restaurant, soaking wet, and I finally managed to convince them that we should be up at the crack of dawn the next morning to make our last attempt at these little French devils.

The lads, nursing bad heads from the night before, staggered out of their rooms on cue and we bundled into the cars for the last time. We arrived at the water's edge before light and sat there with the rain hammering on the roof outside. As it began to get light, we loaded the gear up in the boat and paddled our way to the baited area.

To my delight there were great fizzes of bubbles coming up everywhere. Nine rods covered the baited area and I was soon slipping the net under our first French fish, a mid double that fell to one of Jan's rods.

Moments later, I was away. I just could not believe the power of the carp I had hooked. It took fifty yards of line on its first run. For twenty minutes or so, we did not see the fish. At long last, a cracking common was in the net. On the scales she went 24½lb. At last, after four days of blanking it finally started to happen. During the next six or so hours, between the three of us, we managed to put thirty four fish on the bank, the best of them falling to Chris at 28½lb. We had achieved our goal, all catching twenty pound French commons for the first time. We arrived back at the hotel and even though we were way past our deadline, smiles beamed from our faces and that long, arduous journey back to the ferry did not seem quite the nightmare that it had seemed it was going to be a day or so before.

We went out there with great expectations. I'd really put us on the spot by telling everyone, by putting it in the column, that we were going to the south of France and we were going to stack up all these commons; up until the last day it looked as if I might be emigrating to France because I couldn't face coming home!

We actually cracked it on the last day; we could go home with our heads held high but the troubles began again. That long journey back, right up through France, took its toll on poor old Jan's car. We were in convoy and Chris was in front for most of the time and I was covering the rear. Jan was sandwiched in the middle and his gear box had gone. The problem was, it was leaking oil and this was dripping down onto the exhaust pipe. I was driving in a cloud of smoke right the way back across France, which was rather dodgy to say the least. It was a slow journey, so Chris decided that he would shoot off ahead and go and do a bit of shopping so we agreed to meet him back at the ferry.

We only arrived at the ferry with just minutes to spare and Jan's car died – it finally died as we were going onto the ferry. It was almost a push job to get it on board and my car was absolutely covered in black oil; I

Got one at last!

had to scrape it off the windscreen.

We had rather a rough night's sleep on the ferry across, only to wake up late the next morning. We were almost the last to come off and then, guess what? Jan found he had a flat tyre as well as the other problem, so we had to jack the car up and change the tyre. Then his car wouldn't start so we pushed it onto the dock in England!

That was a holiday to remember, to say the least. It was certainly traumatic, that's for sure.

Willow Park 20 plus common

Getting it right at Old Bury Hill

Jan Wenczka and a French cracker

Praying for a run

23 — Reservoirs and Yateley

That year I ended up at probably one of the most unlikeliest spots for fishing for carp, and that was in the middle of London. There is a vast network of reservoirs at Walthamstow. These are concrete bowls and basically just holes in the ground with water in them but, of course, where there are carp there is an interest.

I was taken there on guest tickets by several people. My old mate, Lenny Middleton, and Kevin Maddocks had fished there in previous years, and they had done quite well. I always remember Lenny saying to me that this one particular reservoir within this group of reservoirs probably holds record carp. That's not something you forget, Lenny wasn't the sort of person to say things lightly, so the opportunity finally came when I could fish there on a guest basis with one of the syndicate members.

The acreage actually increases and decreases on a daily basis. A lot of people who don't fish these types of places, won't realise this.

They are big sheets of water and have enormous depth as well, but no features – this is the problem. There are no bars to look for, or beds of lily pads on these places and there are no pockets of silt or anything. They are big concrete bowls with gravel bottoms.

The one I was fishing is about eighty acres and the depth of water fluctuates by about six feet. It had a depth, when it was full, in excess of forty feet and had a lot of great carp in it which were very difficult to catch, but I'd got the bit between my teeth with these fish, I really had, because you could see them, that was the thing. You didn't have to look for them, you could sit anywhere on this reservoir and they would jump out. The trouble was, they would jump out right in the middle of the reservoir, over forty feet of water and two hundred yards away from you. How on earth do you go about tackling something like that?

It was fascinating, because as well as them being right out in the middle, they were also in the margins. But even in carpet slippers and tiptoeing along as quietly as you possibly could, it was very difficult to get any closer than about fifty yards to these carp without spooking them, let alone casting to them, so here was a major problem. There was no night fishing; there was no admittance before 7.00 a.m. and for most of the year you had to leave between 5 and 6 p.m., so your hours were limited. You were in the middle of London, it was a miserable place to fish, very much affected by the weather. These reservoirs are not in valleys or anything, they are actually built up in the air so they are exposed to all the winds that blow there. You've only got to have the slightest breath of air and you've got a bloomin' gale blowing across these places.

It was a long time before I put a net under one of these carp, I can tell you. Boy, did I struggle there for a long time. I didn't know what to do at first. I thought there could be a chance that when these carp came through in one of the large shoals I might have a hundred carp in front of me. My baiting was not going to be adequate for them. For a start, I had over a mile to walk to get to the reservoir from the car park and I wasn't going to be lugging a couple of hundred pounds of bait, which I would need to stop these carp.

Catching them was going to have to be either by stalking them when they came into the margins, or trying to intercept them with just small patches of bait, or maybe hook baits only, somewhere on the patrol route – both methods failed miserably. It was almost by accident that I eventually twigged how best to catch these fish. When they were rolling right out in the middle of this great depth of water, I studied them with

Lenny Middleton – reservoir advocate

the binoculars for many hours. I couldn't believe that the fish I could see head and shouldering and crashing out were actually going down into forty feet of water. There were times when I had convinced myself that I could see the same fish coming up about thirty seconds after it had previously rolled, which just didn't give it enough time to get down to the bottom.

I couldn't get them to take floaters out there but I thought that I could present bait about ten or fifteen feet below the surface in forty feet of water. This was a problem in itself, because this was quite a considerable range. The closest I could get to those fish was about one hundred yards and when you have got one hundred yards of line out to try and suspend a bait above a big lead in forty feet of water is very difficult to do.

I ended up having to put two large polyballs on the line and use line stops to control the amount of line running through the lead to get these baits towards the surface. When I looked at it I thought, 'this just isn't going to catch carp, it's ridiculous. How can I catch these fish with a floater suspended some ten feet from the surface, four feet below that, two great polyballs. Going a further thirty feet down to a lead, then coming back one hundred yards to the bank'. It looked silly but I thought I'd try it on one rod anyway.

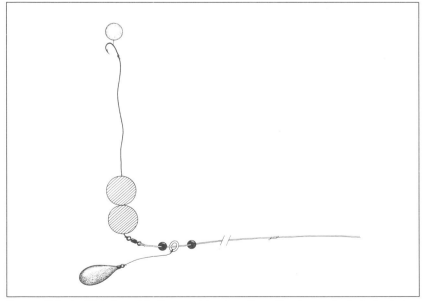

Pop-up fished with twin polyballs – curtain ring allows line to run freely to back stop knot

The conditions were favourable and the fish were within casting range; I managed to chuck this whole really weird conglomerate of a rig out into the middle of the reservoir in the area where I was fishing. I managed to get my bait up because I could feed the line off and I knew it had gone up to the stop and really, I thought that was it – maybe one would be silly enough to hook itself. I just carried on with the other rod.

It had been out there for less than five minutes when it screamed away and after a tremendous battle a twenty seven pounder came on the bank. Although it was very difficult, I did go on and take seven fish out of there in the next three sessions and they were all good twenties right up to 29lb. It was an eye opener for me; these were on single baits, caught in almost a ridiculous manner but it was the depth the carp were at and it worked.

I did return later that winter but only for a few sessions. Again, it was very difficult to get across there and I had to go as a guest, either with other people or with special permission. I went back there on a freezing cold November day. There was flat calm on there, which was rather unusual for the place. Frost everywhere; a lot of waters elsewhere were frozen over.

I went to the area where I had previously seen the fish and I sat there from about 8.00 a.m. onwards after it had taken me a considerable time to walk there in my winter attire. I just couldn't believe they were going to do the same again. I fished out there; I altered the rigs around to fish one five feet below the surface and one ten feet below the surface and I caught three twenties that day, so carp fishing isn't always what it seems to be. It was an eye opener for me – carp caught on a rig that I'd never used before and a tactic that I've never used anywhere before or since.

I was still plodding away at the Shropshire syndicate lake and battling with eels. Those Shropshire eels gave me some stick on the boilies, that's for sure. Several time I tried to fill them in with the hope of feeding the eels off but they just loved them. When you catch an eel of maybe one pound in weight, it's like a pearl necklace. All the boilies have been swallowed whole and they are all inside them.

I went on to fish the chain of Yateley Pits during the winter period. Yateley is one of those waters which, unfortunately, I missed out on, for I should really have fished it in the early eighties. I never got round to it and, of course, by this time it was extremely popular. There were lots of people fishing there, but the Yateley Match Lake, during the course of winter, wasn't quite such a bad proposition.

Chris Ball and I decided that we would get the bait going in there and have a go. We picked a couple of areas, one behind the Dead Tree Island and the other one down by the Copse, between the Twin Islands. We kept bait going in there on a regular basis.

Although we never caught loads of fish, in comparison to what other people caught there, in the short time we were fishing – it was only evenings, there were no nights spent there at all – we did very nicely. We caught a few twenties and found a little bit of peace and quiet on what would normally have been a very busy circuit water. These opportunities are few and far between on heavily fished waters, but occasionally they do arise.

It was a fairly unique situation that Yateley had been busy all summer and had produced a lot of fish, but it became harder during the autumn and the enthusiasm had waned with a lot of anglers and they started disappearing. Of course, we lived so close to Yateley we could easily keep an eye on it and it soon got to the stage where there was very little attention on the Match Lake. For the majority of the time that Chris and I were on there, there were no other carp anglers at all. Just the way we like it!

A good one from Yateley

24 — Redmire

My dreams of a big common did come true when I went to the legendary Redmire Pool. It was great. Redmire was certainly a water that I'd tried to get into on numerous occasions and failed. In some respects this only added to the pool's mystery, for only the very select few were ever invited to fish. However, in 1988 the Carp Society somehow managed to secure the fishing rights at Redmire and things began to change. I was invited to fish the water in October, 1988. I found out as much as I possibly could about catches, bait and tactics that had been successful earlier in the season.

At last the time had come and I set off with high hopes. I had full seven days in which to achieve one of my greatest ambitions – to catch a Redmire carp. Carp Society members Vic Cranfield and Mick Kavanagh were still there. They really had a surprise in store for me, as during the night they had both cracked Redmire Commons, Mick with a double and Vic with a fabulous twenty. I helped them with photographing them before they bade their farewells.

I was shortly joined by Geoff and Paul, who were to be my companions for the next five days. They had both fished Redmire before – Paul was on his second trip whilst Geoff had been a syndicate member for many years. We slowly made our way round the pool and Geoff pointed out all the various swims. To stand where anglers such as Walker, Thomas, Richards and Ingham had fished was really too much to take in.

I wanted to get on with the fishing straight away. It was strange, but when we selected our first spots, thankfully, everyone chose different swims. Geoff was to fish the Willows, Paul the Greenbanks and I settled in the Stumps.

Geoff had quite a knowledge of events that had taken place there over the years. Although carp could be easily seen, cast to one and they would simply melt away. Any noise from the angler's pitch would ensure that they gave it a wide berth.

Bearing this in mind, I thought it would be a good idea to fish nearer the far bank than my own. From the Stumps I could easily cover the margins of Bramble Island, Keffords and the Stile pitch. I decided to use mini boilies and hemp. I selected both a light and a dark bait to see what the response would be, so, armed with a couple of buckets of Crafty Catcher Peanut Pro and Dairy Cream Fudge mini boilies, together with several pounds of cooked hemp, I baited up about half a dozen likely looking gaps in the weed. We were all using different methods. Geoff was using light leads, soft rods and a free running rod end set up. Paul had a real mixture, from the very lightest of leads in his own margin, to a couple of ounce semi-fixed leads for the far bank.

I decided to fish my rods with the tips very high in the air and back-clipped with a very tight line to 1½oz semi fixed lead. The idea was to keep as much line out of the water as possible so that the carp would not come into contact with it. The rig end was a twelve inch length of 8lb BIFA braided terylene, in conjunction with a size 10 or 12 Super Specialist hook, on which one or two mini boilies were hair rigged.

I got my first take just after midnight. This was on my left hand rod to a bait that was positioned just left of the Stile pitch. The fight was nothing spectacular, fairly dogged with the hooked fish weeding itself several times. At last, all my dreams had come true – my first Redmire carp was secure in the folds of the landing net. On the bank, I separated carp from weed and there lay a superb 22¼lb linear mirror. Although I didn't know

Redmire success for all to see

it as the time, I had just landed a carp in excess of fifty years old.

The bait was recast, roughly in position.

Geoff must have heard the commotion and was round at first light to do the honours with the camera. While he was standing in the swim, listening to me relating the earlier events, the same rod sprang to life. The cast couldn't have been that bad after all! Geoff paddled out with the landing net but I had great difficulty in controlling the fish. We could see the fish clearly, a 20lb+ common. Gradually I inched the fish towards the net but just as its nose touched the drawstring, the hook pulled free. Not a word was said; my heart sank.

That was something that was repeated several times during the next few days. I did put a couple of nice, double figure commons on the bank but I lost quite a few other fish. The strange thing was, it always seemed to be the better fish that came adrift, a couple of twenty pound plus commons and a fully scaled mirror were all lost.

The reason for this was that apparently the Redmire carp spend much of their life rooting around in the very soft, rich red mud and over the years have developed an extremely soft and flabby inner skin to the mouth. The combination of the very heavily weeded water and the soft mouth had to be a recipe for problems. Several patterns and sizes of hooks were tried, but all ended up with the hook pulling free. I tried pop ups as there is a ninety five per cent chance of bottom lip hooking with this method, but no takes were forthcoming at all.

The only way I could get takes was to introduce several pounds of bait at a time, on which the carp confidently fed. Geoff, although not encountering any of these problems, hadn't had a take in the whole of his five days there. Paul hadn't fared much better, but did manage to get one double figure common on the first day.

However, they both left very pleased just to have fished the hallowed pool again.

After they left, I moved from the Stumps into the Willows where Geoff had been fishing. The Willow pitch is probably the most famous swim at Redmire and it was from here that Richard Walker caught his magnificent 44lb carp in 1952.

Rods positioned, it was time for a brew up. Just before the kettle had boiled, a screaming take on my left hand rod was the start of a scrappy little fight from a very spirited 13¾lb pristine common. Half an hour or so later, one of its mates at 16lb graced the net. This one tried its hardest to get from the Willows, where I had hooked it, to the Shallows, which is at the opposite end of the lake.

Colin and Alan arrived and they were to fish with me on my final two days at the Mire. We had a good chat and I tried to fill them in with as much info as possible.

What was niggling me, at the back of my mind, was how could I get two takes after moving so soon into the Willows when Geoff had failed all week. It had to be something to do with the set up.

It was just after 5.00 p.m. when I was woken from my thoughts as I bent into another, as yet, unseen fish. I instinctively knew that this would indeed by something special. Slowly, the hooked carp searched the deep water around the dam for sanctuary, picking up weed on the line as it went. Colin came over and I was very grateful that he got the other rods out of the way, which eliminated at least one of the hazards.

After about ten minutes or so, the carp moved from right to left in front of us, some four rod lengths out. It was probably three or four feet under the surface when we caught a glimpse of a huge, golden flank. On the tight line it was forced to the surface and rolled heavily, just to my left. This was indeed something special!

I could not gain any more line because of the weed jammed in the tip ring, so with my arms at full stretch, rod hand way behind me and net hand pushed out as far as I dare, holding on to the very end of the pole,

Heaven!

the carp went in at the first time of asking.

Shaking even more now that it was over, I paddled back to the bank and carp and weed were heaved onto the bank. As Colin and I knelt down either side of the net, separating weed from the fish, there suddenly appeared before us a huge, orange, common carp. Before we even put it on the scales I knew it was going to be a personal best common carp. We checked and rechecked and agreed that the leviathan weighed 29½lb. There were no words that could describe the way I felt – I just let out a victory cry, and leapt and punched my fist in the air, all at the same time!

The light was rapidly fading so between us we carried the common round to the dam and quickly took a few photos before she was returned to her home.

I relived that magic moment time and time again and I eventually drifted off to sleep, but it was a very late breakfast call the next morning. After my late breakfast some time was spent recasting and rebaiting. Around 1.30 p.m. I was away once again. However, after a brief encounter, this one fell foul to the weed and soft mouth syndrome yet again. Not much happened for the rest of the day but as evening drew in the carp began to roll over the baits. I went to bed early and I eventually awoke around seven in the morning, amazed that no takes had been forthcoming.

A quick rebait and recast before breakfast and I would soon have to start thinking about packing up as this was my last morning at Redmire. I was just sorting out my bits and pieces when, to my surprise, my right hand rod was screaming at me again. Soon Alan and Colin were on hand to help out and after another fairly long and determined fight, my second 20lb+ common of the session lay in the bottom of the net. We all recognised it as being one of the famous characters of the pool – the common with no pelvic fins.

At 24lb 7oz this was to be my last Redmire carp and at the very moment we started to take the photographs, the sun shone through for the very first time that week. It seemed to put the crowning glory on a truly memorable week's fishing.

25 — A Change of Attitude

For someone who said they were never going to fish abroad, I was suddenly spending a lot of time there.

On my first trip over there, on the long drive down to the South of France, we did have to pass a lot of waters that I'm sure had loads of carp in them. I wasn't bothered about breaking any records by catching fifty or sixty pounders, it didn't appeal to me. This was something nice during the close season, with a nice bit of sunshine, good food and somewhere to take the wife and kids.

With the help of Roger Sherwood, the owner of Crafty Catcher, we earmarked quite a few other, almost forgotten, waters. These aren't the major waters like St. Cassien or River Lot or River Tarn, but small lakes that are situated on caravan and camp sites, moats round chateaux and all that type of thing. They are reasonably accessible, without that horrendous drive across France, so I decided that we would fish no further south than Tours, in the Loire Valley, where we found this nice lake on a camp site. This water was only about ten acres and I wasn't sure whether or not it had big carp in there, but it certainly had carp for sure, as a lot of these lakes do. It was fairly easy to find out just where, with a few phone calls and by asking the local residents what sort of peche were about. The French eat the carp and you can usually suss out, with just a few odd questions, where the fish are.

We booked this place which was only about four hours drive from Calais, so we arrived there fresh and found that it was actually a holiday camp. The main thing there was camping and water sports other than fishing. There were permanently erected tents, caravans, swimming pool, discos – you name it, it was on the site. Very few English carp anglers had visited this spot so the potential was unknown. This was more of a family holiday than just a fishing trip; because of the disastrous first trip, from the wife's point of view, this had to be a family holiday first and foremost, with the fishing definitely coming second.

Provided I could catch a fish or two during the course of a week's stay, the size and quantity was irrelevant.

The journey was much easier; five hours of steady driving found us unpacking our cases.

Whilst my wife and our younger son, David, were making everything shipshape in the cottage, my elder son, Mark, and I went for a paddle round the lake to get an idea of the lie of the land.

The shape of the lake was something of an uneven 'Y', with about ten feet of water at the deepest end, shallowing off at both arms to about two feet. For the couple of hours that we spent paddling about, small carp showed most of the time. We baited up an area at the junction of the three arms with about 20lb of boilies and dropped out a couple of markers to pinpoint the spot. The weather was marvellous and the temperature was now soaring into the nineties.

The next morning we would have our first crack at carp. We tried various rigs, but anything with a bottom bait on was stripped to shreds in minutes by the abundant crayfish.

Mark and I had gone down to the lake after breakfast and Jeanie and David joined us later. Pop ups fished directly off the lead on a nine inch hook link had an immediate response and, within minutes, a couple of 6lb mirrors were on the bank. Singles and low doubles kept Mark and myself busy for the next couple of hours.

The first cast back in after our lunch of French bread and cheese, and Mark was into a good double. After a cracking scrap I slid the net under a seventeen pounder. This really was exciting stuff, still the small carp kept coming. Mark bent into what was obviously a good fish, which tried its hardest to pull the little lad into the water. We knelt down on either side of a fabulous looking 26lb mirror, a long, lean fighting machine. One or two more mid-doubles saw the end of our first day's carping. As we were on holiday, it was my turn to cook the dinner.

The next day the action was even faster and more furious, so much so, that David and Jeanie had to help out quite a few times when several carp were hooked at once. On the third day I pulled out a real lunker at 35lb 8oz after about a forty minute scrap that had me all over the lake. We also hooked a couple of catfish but only managed to put one on the bank at 2lb. One of them looked to be about six feet long and probably 40 or 50lb!

The tally, after six days' fishing was quite staggering. Between us we had caught in excess of three hundred carp. Around thirty of them were good doubles with eight over 20lb including a couple of thirties. We fished for no more than six hours each day amid some of the most beautiful countryside that France can offer. It was a startling contrast to our first trip to France. There are many of these types of venues scattered throughout France. It is fair to say that you are not going to catch the fifty and sixty pounders of the big French lakes, but with unknown and uncaught fish approaching forty pounds, who really cares? There is a feeling of anticipation every time the indicator flips. It could be 4lb or 40lb. I have been completely converted.

What a lovely place to fish...

26 — Oxford Run

There were some amazing fish from the Oxford Pits. My first venue was a club run ten acre pit within the Windrush watershed. This was a very rich, young pit, with a great deal of potential. It had a fair head of carp, the majority of which were good doubles with maybe fifteen or so twenties and possibly a couple of low thirties.

The second water was much older, a mature gravel pit of about forty five acres, with a very small head of carp, maybe no more than about twenty, and notoriously hard.

We had glorious weather at the start of the season so I concentrated on the smaller club run pits for the first few weeks. I took a number of doubles and six twenties up to 26½lb, the majority of them coming to stalking tactics.

As the weather looked set to change I decided to have a crack at the difficult syndicate pit. I was surprised at just how much weed had sprung up since my first look at it late in the close season. By the beginning of August it was floor to ceiling, with only the odd clear area visible. The fish were difficult to locate but I eventually found a small group of half a dozen or so fish regularly patrolling a particular area of the pit. I heard that only two had been caught by the six or so regulars on the water. However, a few liberal baitings of peanuts and lobster boilies before my first actual fishing session had me chomping at the bit.

The first session produced a string of tench and although there were obviously carp in the vicinity, I do not believe that any picked up the hook baits. The particular area which the carp were patrolling was a series of long bars with fairly narrow troughs in between them and it was in one of these troughs, which was reasonably weed free, that I presented my baits.

To ensure that the casting was spot on, I attached a large polyball, about an inch in diameter, to my hook with some PVA string. I then cast out, sank the line, opened the bail arm to allow the polyball, complete with rig, to rise to the surface. Using this method I could easily see if the cast had been on target. If it had, it was just a matter of tightening up again and sinking the polyball until the PVA string melted. This worked like a dream and as the polyball popped to the surface, I was sure that the bait was in the clear. This does your confidence the world of good. Naturally, the polyballs were retrieved later.

The next session was on the Tuesday of the following week and this time conditions looked a little more favourable. The plan was exactly the same as before; the baits were placed in the tiny weed free areas of the trough, between the mainline with an ounce and a half running lead and a ten inch length of 15lb breaking strain Silkworm. To the end of this was attached a size 6 Super Specialist hook and a short mid shank tied hair on which was mounted an 18mm diameter bottom bait. The hook baits were joined by several hundred free offerings.

A carp rolled over very close to the baited area; I just knew I was going to catch, and my instinct did not let me down, for in the early hours of the morning a screaming take had me bent into my first fish from this hard water. I ended up going in for it and after a bit of a battle, the prize was mine – an exceedingly long linear mirror of 25lb plus – what a magic moment.

The next session was fairly uneventful, save for the tench again. In actual fact, I couldn't find the carp at all. It was on the next Monday evening when I was looking round for fish to have a crack at on the following night. The conditions had completely changed, there was now a very strong south westerly wind really blowing a gale. As I stood on the windward side of the bank a large carp head and shouldered in the margins, right at my feet and almost had me going home for my tackle. However, I decided to sit there and see if I could spot any more, and during the next couple of hours at least six more fish showed. I gave the swim a good baiting up before returning home.

The following evening I returned and by now, the wind had reached gale force and was positively crashing into my bank. I made everything ready for the night and although everything looked right, I was in no hurry; after all, I didn't want to make any mistakes. This time there was no casting involved as the baits were fished just a couple of rod lengths out.

By now there were huge rafts of weed building up in the margins of the swim and it was continually getting snagged up with the line. Fortunately, this was quite easily overcome. I dropped the rod tips so that they were below the water and put a second back lead on to ensure that the line went along the bottom before vertically coming up to the rod tips.

A couple of the regulars dropped in for a chat and a cup of tea. Most of the talk centred around the big mirror that was resident in the lake and I remember remarking that I was sure it was not a million miles away.

They wished me luck and bade me farewell.

About midnight the right hand rod screamed; there were no preliminary bleeps or anything. I don't know which was louder, the screech of the Optonic or my poor old 300 S's trying to keep up with one very speedy, irate carp!

There was no point in trying to strike, or even grab the handle, I just let the fish run for probably twenty or thirty yards. As I tried to gain some line it kited way round to my left hand side and momentarily became bogged down in heavy weed. I pumped like mad to get it moving, which sent the carp tearing off on yet another long run. By now it was seventy odd yards up to my left, but at least it had slowed down.

The best idea was to move along the bank and try to gain line on the hooked fish, so dragging my landing net behind me, I moved myself round most of the bankside obstacles. The carp was not moving and the line was solid with weed. I was beginning to get a bit worried, for no matter what I did, the carp remained stationary. There was only one thing for it – I would just have to go in.

I waded straight in, fully clothed and it was only then that I realised just how strong the wind was, as the waves crashed against my chest. Fortunately, I had only gone ten or fifteen yards out when the carp began to move.

It was now like a completely different fish, covered in weed and I easily steered it into the net. As I parted the weed from the fish, it was obviously a good one, perhaps a low thirty. On the scales it proved to be just a couple of ounces short of the magic thirty but I was certainly more than pleased.

I quickly changed my clothes and took some photos with my camera set up on the tripod. About the third frame in, the left hand indicator signalled the start of another battle.

I quickly slipped the twenty nine back into the water and bent into another lively carp. Although this was a very spirited fight, it was all over in a matter of minutes, but at 21lb there was no way I was going to complain. A brace of twenties before 1 o'clock in the morning was great news indeed and a celebratory cup of tea was called for.

With rods repositioned, I finally got into my sleeping bag and I really thought that would be my lot for the night but, to my amazement, only a few yards away from me a good carp crashed out.

I drifted off to sleep but was woken with a start by the left hand Optonic singing again. Not bothering with shoes or anything I jumped straight out of bed and bent into the fish. Immediately, I knew this was

Bally cracked it

What a lovely common

Perfect linear

29.08 of common

A whacker in Andy's lad's arms

35.08 of French lunker

The Oxford 36.10

something different.

It slowly and determinedly plodded away to the right – the power was unbelievable – no amount of sidestrain was going to stop it. The unseen monster continued to gain line from my right hand and then kited in. I knew I was really going to be in trouble now as further down the bank was a small peninsula with a large, snaggy bush overhanging the water. I tried with all my might to turn the fish before it reached it, but the sound of cracking branches made me realise that I had failed. Fortunately, the carp was still well and truly hooked, although the line was snagged in the branches, so the second dip of the night was on the cards.

The water under the bush was fairly shallow and with not too many problems I managed to free the snagged line. The carp was very patient with all this and just wallowed about on a tight line ten feet or so on the other side of the bush. Once the line was in the clear I made my way back to the bank from where I played the fish out under the rod tip for perhaps five minutes. I caught sight of a huge flank as it rolled into the net. That was enough to know that I had caught a big 'un.

I tried to weigh the big mirror but was shaking too much – whether it was from the cold, or excitement, I don't know – but it appeared to be about 37lb! I changed my clothes yet again and now, free from the shakes, I weighed the fish at 36lb 10oz, my third largest English carp. What a sight to see as it swam strongly away into the gin clear water of its home.

27 — Bulgaria

Since working for D.A.M. my lifestyle has changed quite considerably as it involves travelling throughout the Continent on a regular basis. Of course this opportunity has given me the chance to fish many new waters throughout France, Germany, Holland, Belgium and beyond. It has often been said that this globe trotting carp fishing would spoil things here in the U.K., but in fact that is not the case at all. I still have the same drive and enthusiasm as ever and there is always that exclusive forty pounder to fish for here in England. I have been fortunate to catch fish within a few ounces of that magic weight and several of these have since far exceeded forty pounds. Who knows one day I may well bump into one of those fish again. I suppose I would by lying if I said I wasn't slightly envious of people who have caught forties here in the U.K. but generally speaking so much time is needed to camp out on hard waters if you are going to be successful targeting one of these real large carp. That is of course unless you have an exclusive syndicate with one of these megafish swimming around in it – which I certainly have not. I don't want to knock people who set their stall out for one of the Yateley monsters or similar, I actually admire their singlemindedness and determination but I'm afraid it's not for me.

I'm glad to say quite a few forty pounders have come my way, not from England but from abroad.

The first was a forty one pounder from France, in fact from St. Cassien. I have also taken another from that water since as well as one from Saligou and another from a mid French water and so it goes on. All those fish were very pleasing and probably meant no less to me than any fish I have caught from England. In fact there is one catch that springs to mind from a recent trip that I consider almost one of my best angling achievements. Not because of any clever method I used or from a particularly strong fight that I had won but for eventually conquering many other outside problems that I encountered before a couple of Bulgarian forties finally graced my net.

It was about a year ago that I started the search after tracing some stockings that had taken place in the late forties. These were the beginnings of a commercial fishing network that has now spread throughout many rivers and lakes in Bulgaria. After a lot of groundwork it looked like some of these carp have actually grown to quite massive proportions but my Bulgarian contact revealed that there was much red tape I would have to get through to enable me to wet a line. In fact he suggested at one stage that some of the better waters that were normally in inaccessible areas of the country were virtually going to be impossible. But he had now wetted my appetite and I had seen photos with my own eyes so I was not to be beaten, I just had to keep pursuing the possibilities. A stroke of luck came via Tim Meadows of Anglers' Abroad here in England. Tim and one of his colleagues also knew some people in authority out in Bulgaria so plans for a trip were made – not for fishing but just to go and explore the possibilities. This was really frustrating. We were taken and shown all sorts of good looking waters but trying to get across to them the fact that we wanted to come over and fish for their carp with rod and line and return them once landed seemed to be almost impossible. And, judging from the comments that were made the people in authority there really must have thought that we were quite crazy. After all the only reason anyone fishes in Bulgaria was for food. The idea of going to all the trouble of flying out there, spending hours on the bank to catch a fish or two just to photograph them, seemed unbelievably ludicrous to our hosts. But eventually after lots of meetings with the local hierarchy we were given permission to fish.

A few weeks later, accompanied by a small band of friends, I went out on the first exploratory trip. This was an absolute disaster; we caught loads and loads of carp, most of them being singles with just the odd double to about sixteen pounds. It looks like they had bred so prolifically that it was going to be impossible to select the larger fish that were undoubtedly there. The disappointment of so much hard work almost destroyed the thought of trying again but I felt there should be a lake available somewhere that would give me a better opportunity of catching some of the larger carp that I felt existed on many of these Bulgarian waters.

Not to be beaten, once back in the U.K. the correspondence started yet again and some good news came through from a completely different part of the same country. This was from a fish-farm down on the Black Sea border in the area of Bourgas. Here there was a vast network of lakes covering many thousand of acres where commercial fishing was taking place. but the best news was that the larger fish were of little or no use for selling on as they were deemed too large for good eating. It would appear that only carp up to about 20 pounds were taken, many of the others were returned. Can you imagine my delight when I was greeted with this sort of news? This was also backed up with some more photographs of what appeared to be some very large fish. Well that was it, hasty plans were made and once again we were off to Bulgaria.

Much time had now elapsed and it was now October which was out of the normal scheduled flight season so we ended up having to travel through Austria and then Sofia, the capital of Bulgaria, and eventually via a local flight onto Bourgas. Arriving again there was the normal red tape to go through. Having put our case forward time and time again to many people in authority, the whole project was a continuing series of highs and lows. Many days passed with little happening and I often wondered whether it was worth pursuing. But eventually I was taken to a lake which in fact wasn't a lake, it was just a bay that was part of an enormous five thousand acre sheet of water that had been cordoned off from a road that had been pushed through several years ago. It was apparently in this huge bay that a lot of the bigger fish had been returned. I stood on one of the only accessible points on this reed fringed water and was confronted with carp moving everywhere. It looked like no one had been there for years, certainly no sport fishing had ever taken place and there were no swims as such. The only vantage point was a small slipway where I could gain access. This was used by the fish farmers in years gone by. It was here that I set up.

Because of all the meetings I now only had realistically a couple of days in which to fish before catching the return flight home. I had little in the way of bait as the strict baggage allowance only left room for three bags of 18mm Tutti Frutti boilies. The rest of my 15 kilos allowance was made up of a pump up lilo replacing the normal bedchair, a small lightweight one-man tent and a light summer sleeping bag. All that lot went in one bag as hold luggage. On board as hand luggage went my camera, three F.S. 350 reels, a set of buzzers and a box of terminal tackle. Also to ensure that my rods got there undamaged, unlike on previous trips, I now use D.A.M. Telescopic Carp Rods. This together with landing net, rod pod and a two piece specially converted landing net handle also went on board with me as my second piece of hand baggage.

Having sorted out where to fish I had a quick chat with the local farmer/manager who amazingly instantly produced a big bag of barley and maize. This his wife set about cooking for me and great big buckets of the stuff were kindly delivered to my swim. Their hospitality was just marvellous and the manager even helped paddle his boat out for me to bait up. This I did at about 25 yards out into the swim and put in even amounts of barley and maize. I was fishing over about 8 feet of water and set up all three rods on very basic free running rigs. These were fished in conjunction with quite large hooks of size 2. To this I hair rigged a couple of boilies on the first rod, three on the second and four on the third, the idea being to give these very naive carp a good mouthful of food tempting them to pick them up. Considering they had never seen boilies before in their life I got quite a surprise when only after a quarter of an hour I was bent into my first fish. Having never seen a hook or angler before the upper twenty common went off like a train. As that fish went over the net I thought at last after all the months of hard work perhaps I had really found what I was looking for and maybe things were now going to go my way. That they certainly did! Throughout the day takes came very regularly and at one stage I could not cope with fish on all three rods at the same time. By midnight I was completely shattered, arms aching from continually playing fish, I just had to stop fishing and get some sleep.

I woke at around six, baited up and cast out – the action was just as intense as on that first day. The swim had very little in the way of snags and although every fish hooked fought like a tiger I actually did not lose anything at all. On the second day I landed a fantastic 41lb 12oz carp. This was undoubtedly the most exciting fishing that I had ever experienced.

By 10 o'clock in the evening I was once again exhausted. I got my head down for a few hours but was up again at first light just to get the last couple of hours fishing in before heading for the airport.

The statistics of the catch were mind blowing as in the two days and half nights 65 carp had graced my net. Fifty of these were over 20 pounds and their weights were broken down as follows: 39 of them were between 20 and 30 pounds; 9 between 30 and 40 pounds and 2 over 40 pounds, a common of 41lb 12oz and a mirror of 42lb. By far the larger percentage were commons, looking completely different to those we find here in the U.K. These were extremely deep, solid and very broad fish. They looked very young and fast growing. I'm sure there were much larger fish in the swim to be caught – monsters maybe 70 or 80 pounds would occasionally leap clear of the water but time was not on my side. With so many large fish in the swim it was just impossible to be any more selective. I also had three silver carp which are plankton eaters and imported from Russia to keep the algae level down in the lakes. Even these picked up boilies. The largest of these was 75lb but quite honestly this was just a baby as they exist in excess of 200lb in this area of Bulgaria.

I really can't wait to get back.

I completely enjoy this pioneering type fishing. It is a great substitute for new ventures here in the U.K. where it almost seems that virtually

Andy's first Bulgarian carp; an upper twenty

every bit of water here has been exploited.

I know many people will say it's not the same but to me it's all relative, it's what I personally feel at the time. I enjoy carp fishing wherever it may be and relish the opportunity of fishing new countries and meeting new friends. Hopefully this will carry on for as many years as I am capable of doing it.

It's certainly nice to be able to put something back into a sport that has given me so much pleasure as hopefully through my writings it will encourage other people to follow the same sort of pattern. The world is literally our oyster. Carp are spread far and wide throughout the world and travel is so much cheaper and easier.

For the future I just want to carry on carp fishing and enjoying it as I do now, and watching my two young sons Mark and David getting the same sort of enjoyment, following in my footsteps just as I did in my father's.

These were wild fish that had never seen a hook before

A typical high backed fat, fast growing Bulgarian common

Just one last 20 before it's time to catch the plane

Five 30lb plus commons from Bulgaria. All the fish were caught in short succession and retained only for a minimal length of time